Advance Praise for
The Anticipatory Organization

"If you're in business, and you're not thinking about disruption, you're not paying attention. And if you haven't read *The Anticipatory Organization*, you haven't learned how to think about—and get ahead of—the disruption that's headed your way. Read this book!"

—Alan M. Webber, Cofounder, *Fast Company*

"Daniel Burrus's new book, *The Anticipatory Organization*, provides critical insights into trends shaping the future of business. Burrus delivers a powerful vision for driving growth and innovation within a company. This is a must-read for emerging digital leaders within any industry."

—Jude Schramm, CIO, General Electric Company, Aviation

"*The Anticipatory Organization* provides a compelling methodology to enable each of us to identify future trends and meaningful opportunities in a time of hyper change. Simple in its approach, yet truly transformational in its results."

—Joel Doherty, Head of Global Strategy and
Business Development, EPSON Cloud/EPSON America

"Ever since we introduced your Anticipatory Organization concepts to our leaders and managers, our ability to solve complex problems has dramatically improved. We commonly talk about Hard Trends and Soft Trends and how defining them gives our planning efforts certainty in the uncertain world of healthcare. *The Anticipatory Organization* is a must-read for every leader!"

—Roger Spoelman, Regional President and CEO,
Trinity Health/Mercy Health

"New disruptions are constantly changing industries. But with *The Anticipatory Organization* in hand, you now have a choice: disruptor or disrupted? That's a power advantage—and this is a must-read for every brand."

—Andrew Vesey, Founder and Coeditor, *Brand Quarterly* magazine

"In the 21st century, leaders can't merely react to transformational change; they need a disciplined model for anticipating and shaping the future. *The Anticipatory Organization* provides a compelling model that helps shift leaders' mind-sets from reactive to proactive, and empowers them to impact the future with skill and certainty."

—Doug Conant, former President, Nabisco Foods Company; former President and CEO, Campbell Soup Company; former Chairman, Avon Products; *New York Times* best-selling author; founder, Conant Leadership

"*The Anticipatory Organization* teaches you how to elevate your planning based on the Hard Trends that are shaping the future, and how to accelerate your results. It is a must-read for any organization that is experiencing increased competition and an uncertain future."

—Terry Halvorsen, former CIO Department of Defense, EVP Samsung Electronics

"Daniel Burrus offers readers a road map on how to think and act differently. *The Anticipatory Organization* teaches you how to accelerate both everyday innovation as well as exponential innovation throughout the entire organization."

—William J. Bender, Lt. General, CIO, United States Air Force

"*The Anticipatory Organization* teaches you how to accelerate growth by jumping ahead of the competition with low risk. It's a must-read for anyone who wants an edge on tomorrow."

—Kevin Harrington, serial entrepreneur; original shark on *Shark Tank*; and cofounder of the Entrepreneurs' Organization

"Finally, a guide to creating an anticipatory, innovative culture capable of getting ahead and staying ahead in these disruptive times. *The Anticipatory Organization* will show you how to transform your organization for success, create an anticipatory culture capable of both everyday innovation and game-changing, exponential innovation. A must-read for every leader looking for a competitive advantage."

—Tom Hood, CEO of the Business Learning Institute

"As an inventor and innovator, it is always refreshing to find a new take on innovation. Dan's new book can help you sift through current trends to find those most likely to happen and give your organization confidence to make bold moves."

—Terry Jones, Founder of Travelocity.com, Founding Chairman, Kayak.com, and author of *ON Innovation*

"*The Anticipatory Organization* is a must-read book for planning, decision-making, and growing the bottom line. Burrus has prepared a detailed flight plan to assist organizations of all sizes in gaining altitude and avoiding a lot of turbulence."

—Howard Putnam, Former CEO, Southwest Airlines, and author of *The Winds of Turbulence*

"The future doesn't need to be nearly as unpredictable as we fear. Whether we work in a large organization or a one-person shop, Daniel Burrus shows us in highly practical terms what's coming next, and what leaders must do right now to get ready for it. Act on this wisdom before your competition does."

—John R. Ryan, President and CEO, Center for Creative Leadership

"Daniel Burrus is one of the brightest and most innovative people I know. *The Anticipatory Organization* explores solid strategies that can propel you, your team, and your business in significant ways. Read it. Discuss it. Apply it. Benefit from it."

—Dr. Nido R. Qubein, President, High Point University

"*The Anticipatory Organization* teaches readers how to go beyond being agile to truly being anticipatory by understanding future facts that can lead to seizing unseen opportunities. This book is a game changer if you want to be a disruptor rather than disrupted. Truly a future-ready mind-set—love it!"   —Joey Havens, Executive Partner, Horne LLP

"Daniel Burrus offers a unique perspective and critical insights on anticipating digital disruption and provides unprecedented advice to stay ahead of the technological curve. If you'd like to drive innovation and growth within your company while minimizing risk, *The Anticipatory Organization* is a must-read."   —Anoop N. Mehta, President, SSAI

"Reacting to disruption and change is getting harder every year. Learning how to see change coming before it arrives by becoming anticipatory turns change into your biggest competitive advantage. *The Anticipatory Organization* does this and far more. Read it today!"

—Greg Kammer, EVP, Strategy, Retail and Sales Operations, Ashley Furniture Industries

"Putting out fires and managing the crisis of the moment are important, but pre-solving predictable problems or skipping them all together is far better. The strategies and principles in *The Anticipatory Organization* can directly benefit both your business life as well as your personal life."

—Barbara Nollau, Executive Director, Amgen

"There is no shortage of trends. The problem is: Which ones will happen? *The Anticipatory Organization* teaches you how to separate the Hard Trends, that will happen, from the Soft Trends, that might happen—giving you and your organization the confidence to make bold moves."

—Joel Portice, CEO, Intermedix

"*The Anticipatory Organization* shows you how to find certainty in an uncertain world and use the confidence that comes from certainty to jump ahead of the competition and stay ahead."

—Jack Canfield, coauthor of *The Success Principles* and the best-selling Chicken Soup for the Soul book series, and CEO, The Canfield Training Group

"In an era of exponentially increasing complexity, *The Anticipatory Organization*'s simple approach to identifying future trends and innovation is a breath of fresh air."

—Derek A. Bang, CPA, CGMA, Chief Strategy & Innovation Officer, Crowe Horwath LLP

"Daniel Burrus's new book, *The Anticipatory Organization*, empowers you with the planning and transformational tools you need to leverage change, turn disruption into opportunity, and ensure the future happens with you—not to you."

—Alan D Whitman, CPA, CGMA, Chairman and CEO, Baker Tilly

"*The Anticipatory Organization* is an incredibly logical, practical, and easy-to-read tool kit for any business leader driven to shift their firm to the highest levels of success by embracing an anticipatory mindset—a mindset that "anticipates solutions at the speed of need."

—Risa Lavine, Chief of Staff, CohnReznick

"*The Anticipatory Organization* uncovers a new model for planning, innovation, and problem-solving. It lays out simple and workable tactics to explore possibilities from predicable future realities. Mr. Burrus identifies a model that creates a mindset of opportunities that can move your company, department, and even your personal career forward exponentially. It puts employees on their toes with anticipation, rather than on the heels of their routine. *The Anticipatory Organization* is an easy, quick read that I would recommend for those leaders who are working on strategy, innovation, and looming industry shifts."

—Tom Pratt, Director of Organizational Development,
ScanSource Inc.

"*The Anticipatory Organization* challenges readers to think differently—about their assumptions, about their opportunities, and about perceived hurdles. The concepts in this book can easily apply to individuals as well as to organizations in terms of developing capabilities to innovate using Hard and Soft Trend methodologies. Dr. Burrus challenges long-standing notions about change curves and points out that there is no time like the present to seize opportunities. With an AO Mindset, the future is an exciting place!"

—Kim Fields, VP, JM Family Enterprises

THE
ANTICIPATORY
ORGANIZATION

THE ANTICIPATORY ORGANIZATION

Turn Disruption and Change into Opportunity and Advantage

Based on an Award-Winning Learning System
that Has Changed How Leading Companies Plan and Innovate

DANIEL BURRUS

author of seven books including *The New York Times* and *Wall Street Journal*
bestseller *Flash Foresight* and the highly acclaimed *Technotrends*

GREENLEAF
BOOK GROUP PRESS

Published by Greenleaf Book Group Press
Austin, Texas
www.gbgpress.com

Distributed by Greenleaf Book Group

For ordering information or special discounts for bulk purchases, please contact Greenleaf Book Group at PO Box 91869, Austin, TX 78709, 512.891.6100.

Cover design by Miroslav Jolic
Design and composition by Greenleaf Book Group

Cover Image ©Rawpixel, 2017.
Used under license from Shutterstock.com
Author Photography by James Bareham

Cataloging-in-Publication data is available.

Print ISBN: 978-1-62634-446-4

eBook ISBN: 978-1-62634-447-1

Part of the Tree Neutral® program, which offsets the number of trees consumed in the production and printing of this book by taking proactive steps, such as planting trees in direct proportion to the number of trees used: www.treeneutral.com

TreeNeutral®

Printed in the United States of America on acid-free paper

20 21 22 23 24 25   13 12 11 10 9 8 7 6 5 4

First Edition

To my wife, my soul mate, my best friend, and biggest fan, Sharon: You are a constant source of love and inspiration.

And to the millions of people around the world who have been in my audiences, read my books, and have taken action on the ideas that I sparked in their minds: It is your positive actions that fuel my passion for continuing to inspire you to shape a better tomorrow.

And to the thousands of leaders around the world who have shared their amazing experiences of applying the principles of our Anticipatory Organization Learning System to transform their organizations and results: You were the inspiration to write this book.

CONTENTS

Introduction

A well-known expression tells us that the future holds only two certainties—death and taxes, not necessarily in that order.

Today, this dangerous misconception can get you into trouble fast. Let's face it: Moving exponentially faster in the wrong direction can prove to be a major problem or downright disastrous, as evidenced by the many digital startups—not to mention Fortune 500 companies—that have either failed or fallen off the 500 list.

The future is far more certain than you realize—and knowing where to find certainty in an uncertain world provides a big advantage for those who have learned how and where to look. I'm very excited that you're seeking more effective ways to shape the future—before someone else does it for you.

The Anticipatory Organization book—inspired by the dramatic results organizations are obtaining from our learning system of the same name—offers a comprehensive new way to identify the game-changing opportunities you and your organization can uncover by employing a completely new model of thinking, planning, innovating, and taking action based on anticipation.

Using the principles of this acclaimed Anticipatory Organization Model, you will learn how to identify those trends and other factors that will drive an amazing number of predictable future events—and, from there, to plan accordingly to pinpoint and act upon the enormous opportunities of tomorrow and pre-solve problems before they occur.

Digital transformation divides all of us into two camps—the disruptor and the disrupted. *The Anticipatory Organization* gives you a choice! Disruption will happen, but when you learn how to see it coming, you have a choice to either be the disrupted or the disruptor.

Agility Is Valuable, but You Will Need More than That!

Organizations of all types and sizes have traditionally relied on their ability to react as quickly as possible to shifting challenges, the demands of the marketplace, and other types of disruptions. That's often referred to as agility.

Being agile is very important, but it is simply no longer good enough. We are living in an era of accelerating disruption—not simple change, but outright transformational change. Revolutionary technology and business concepts are rendering traditional systems and modes of thinking less relevant and even obsolete at an increasing pace.

If you or your organization were looking to leverage that sort of transformative growth, would you rather have merely reacted as quickly as possible as change took place or anticipated it and crafted well-thought-out plans to take full advantage of its game-changing opportunities?

The Imperative of a New Model

In just a few short years, 90 percent of the global population will be covered by mobile broadband networks, and 70 percent will be using a smartphone. The explosive growth of smartphones and Internet access illustrates the rate of change we're experiencing now—one whose speed is only going to increase exponentially in the future. And it's not just a matter of identifying and making the most of all sorts of opportunities. Change and disruption can also bring problems. As those, too, come at an ever faster rate, will you be able to react and keep your head above water, let alone take advantage of the opportunities that rapid change can offer?

It's clear that a new model is necessary—one based on anticipation and not just fast reaction.

As this book will discuss, an Anticipatory Organization uses predictable Hard Trends to anticipate disruptions, problems, and industry-shifting opportunities before they occur, allowing them to turn disruption and change into opportunities and advantage. By understanding how to separate predictable Hard Trends that *will* happen from Soft Trends that *might* happen, leaders can elevate plans and use exponential tools to accelerate innovation that will drive transformational results.

Can we predict everything? Of course not. But we can predict more than enough to make a very real difference in how we plan to meet the future. If you change the way you think, you can change the results of what you do.

A Model for Everyone

Although this book is titled *The Anticipatory Organization*, don't interpret that to relate only to massive companies. The Anticipatory Organization Model is just as powerful for individuals and small groups as it is for larger organizations. Moreover, these anticipatory skills and strategies can be used by all members of an organization to build an environment characterized by innovation, collaboration, and a confident, shared view of the future.

That's why I'm so excited that you're reading this book. That means that you share my passion about shaping a positive future and that you're eager to be as proactive as possible about crafting that future.

I'm also excited to know that you are interested in exploring my conviction that organizations that employ anticipatory thinking will be positioned to identify and leverage the remarkable opportunities of tomorrow—opportunities shaped by a dynamic environment. This book will show you how to become one of those game-changing organizations.

KNOW WHAT'S NEXT—
TRANSFORM PLANNING

Chapter 1

Disproving a Dangerous Misconception

Apple sold a billion iPhones in ten short years—a phone that has taken more pictures than any other camera in the world. Canon, Nikon, and Olympus certainly never saw that coming.

Would your organization have spotted the disruption those companies missed? Could you have developed a plan to profit from that disruption?

How did Uber devise a revolutionary taxi service without owning a single vehicle? Netflix is the largest movie theater on the planet—how were they able to develop a plan to achieve that without owning even one movie house? How did Mark Zuckerberg have the confidence to turn down Yahoo's offer of one billion dollars to buy Facebook—and go on to develop the world's most popular social networking site without creating a sliver of original content?

Why didn't a cab driver think of Uber? Why didn't massive hospitality companies such as Marriott and Hilton come up with the billion-dollar concept used by Airbnb? What methodology made those sorts of game-changing innovations not just possible but viable? Does your organization know what it is? Does it know how to drive Exponential Innovation with relatively low risk just as Uber, Netflix, and Facebook did?

What competency are you missing?

In framing those questions, it's understandable to talk about certain traditional competencies that many consider essential to business success and growth—execution, maintaining a lean operation, and working toward zero defects, among others. In particular, the most recent is a focus on being agile: In trying to manage the increasing pace of disruption and change, the ability to react faster than the competition is the silver bullet.

Netflix excelled in its strategy of beating Blockbuster by mailing DVDs to its customers. Had they continued with just that, however, they would have missed a bigger opportunity: video streaming. Did their ability to execute at a high level enable them to identify and act on an even greater disruptive opportunity? The answer is no. Companies that disrupt an industry don't rely on traditional strategies and competencies that other organizations use every day.

Companies large and small that turn an entire industry on its ear have developed "the missing competency": a learnable skill to anticipate the future with remarkable accuracy, make decisions with greater confidence, and drive exponential, disruptive innovation with much lower risk and high levels of certainty in a world where uncertainty dominates.

The Missing Competency: The Ability to Anticipate

Ask yourself:

- What if you could see disruptions before they impacted your career, organization, and industry?

- What if you could accelerate innovation with far greater certainty and much lower risk?

- What if you could predict problems and solve them before they happened?

- What if you were able to establish a culture of incremental and exponential innovation in your organization?

Would finding the answers to these questions give you a personal and professional advantage? The answer, obviously, is a resounding yes. Who among us wouldn't embrace the opportunity to move beyond the frustrating struggle of merely reacting and responding?

You can learn to anticipate the future with more than enough accuracy to allow you to make decisions and plans with a high degree of certainty and much lower risk. Even better, learning to be anticipatory elevates skills and competencies you're already familiar with. Consider the following:

- Would an ability to predict and pre-solve problems help you take your lean initiatives to the next level?

- If you could forecast the future with a high level of accuracy, would that naturally make your organization more agile?

- Would the ability to anticipate your customers' future problems allow you to develop low-risk products and services at the "speed of need?"

- Would pre-solving product problems naturally boost efforts to be as defect-free as possible?

Many will dismiss the ability to accurately forecast the future as a one-time epiphany that only those fortunate few—the Zuckerbergs and the Steve Jobs of the world—are mystically graced to experience. Maybe you're one of them: "I'm a businessperson. I'm not Jeff Bezos. I'm not Mark Zuckerberg. I can't see what those other guys saw. And those things only happen once in a lifetime."

To which I reply: "You're mistaken. The fact that you can catch an

Uber to enjoy an evening at an Airbnb disproves the idea that only a few can anticipate the future. You can, too—if you know how."

This book is dedicated to sharing the process I've developed and shared with CEOs and top leaders throughout the world who have learned to turn change and disruption into advantage. It's called The Anticipatory Organization Model™ (or AO Model) and I'm going to show you how and why you can use it to transform the future of your organization.

Step One: The Base of the Mountain

We are living in a time of accelerating digital disruption—not mere change, but game-changing, transformational change. Revolutionary technology and business concepts are everywhere, rendering traditional systems and modes of thinking less relevant and often obsolete.

Moreover, all this extraordinary disruption and transformation is just getting started. We're only at square one, the base of the mountain. And what once might have been a gradual slope of 45 degrees has sharpened to the point where innovation is taking place at a vertical incline. Unfortunately, our path up the mountain is shrouded by the fog of the issues and events of the moment. An Anticipatory Mindset allows you to see through the fog and identify the opportunities most will miss.

Consider: It took 32 years from the time the zipper was invented until the technology was in place to actually allow something to be zipped up. Television took 29 years from invention to production—the transistor, ten years. These are examples of technology-driven innovation and change, of course, but at a time when tech-driven change was so slow that reacting and responding to change worked quite well. There was little in the way of rapid disruption.

We aren't experiencing that tortoiselike rate of change anymore. The pace of change is getting exponentially faster every day and is literally changing the world on a daily basis. Need proof? In 2015, at a gathering in Toronto, 200 people and myself were treated to a meal created by a rather unusual chef—the IBM cognitive supercomputer, Watson.

In order to craft a meal that all of us would love, Watson read—and more importantly *learned*—the contents of more than a million cookbooks and everything that has been written about the sense of taste and smell. How long did it take Watson to do all this? One second! And that was a few years ago. It's an absolute certainty that Watson will be able to do the same thing even faster in the years ahead.

Wondering how a computer like Watson could benefit your organization (beyond culinary matters)? A year later, I delivered a speech to the annual partners meeting of the international audit, tax, and advisory firm KPMG LLP, where I shared my Toronto experience. As part of my remarks, I suggested that the company apply Watson to the world of auditing and taxes by learning the entire tax code and using it in all sorts of innovative ways. This would allow KPMG to provide a new level of service to their clients—and if they didn't do it, someone else would. The company is now implementing plans to use Watson's cognitive prowess to analyze and interpret enormous amounts of financial and tax data that no human being could possibly manage.

Watson is just one example of the explosive type of disruptive change and innovation we're experiencing. Unlike cyclic change, which repeats like the swing of a pendulum, this is a form of linear, one-way change that forms an exponential curve. Once it occurs, there's no going back. You don't have a multimillion-dollar supercomputer in a room in your home, but you can use a supercomputer anytime you want when you use your smartphone or tablet to conduct a search or ask Siri, Google Now, or Alexa a question. With a supercomputer right in the palm of your hand, linear, flat, one-way change morphs into exponential change.

Change and disruption are also coming from unlikely sources. Whether it's a solitary hacker in some distant location breaching a corporate or government firewall or a college kid who devises an industry-changing mobile app, disruption can now come from the most modest, unexpected sources. To quote *The Economist*: Newcomers can "incorporate online for a few hundred dollars, raise money from crowdsourcing sites such as Kickstarter, hire programmers from Upwork, rent computer-processing power from Amazon, find manufacturers on Alibaba, arrange payments via Square, and immediately set about conquering the world."[1]

You can be one of those game changers. By learning to use the predictability of cyclical change, as well as one-way linear and exponential change, you can see the future with far more accuracy. The environment we're living in is bursting with both opportunity and a good deal of danger—the kinds of danger that can disrupt your industry, business, or career almost overnight.

Struggle, Then Struggle Some More

My work as an innovation expert and professional futurist allows me to work closely with a wide variety of companies, governments, agencies, and organizations. Many of the largest and most resourceful have shared that they are struggling to keep up—even those that were icons at one time.

Known for its ability to execute, Dell was once the world's number one computer company. However, the company missed the shift to mobile and has struggled to catch up ever since. The heart of the company's business—PCs, laptops, and netbooks—became less relevant as consumers and businesses shifted toward smartphones, tablets, and wearables.

Hewlett-Packard took much the same track as Dell. In addition to the steady decline of HP's PC and printer businesses over the past number of years, cloud computing—Internet-hosted remote servers to store, manage, and process data—grew, taking a major chunk out of

---

1   "Reinventing the Company," *The Economist*, October 24, 2015, p. 9.

HP's data center equipment sales. Both Dell and HP are now racing to catch up—an increasingly difficult task as change and disruption grow faster all the time.

In the world of mobile phones, Motorola was once a major brand. They *invented* the mobile phone in the early eighties and were the first to dramatically reduce its size with the StarTAC, the first clamshell, or flip phone, in 1996. But like many other industry standard-bearers, they are no longer shaping the future.

INDUSTRY DOESN'T HAVE A MONOPOLY ON THIS STRUGGLE JUST TO KEEP UP

Governments around the world have moved even slower on a number of important issues. For instance, in 2015, Amazon and other companies started working toward comprehensive product delivery services using drones. Meanwhile, the US federal government scrambled to devise applicable safety regulations. As of early 2016, the only regulation implemented was a law requiring drones of a minimum size and weight to have a registration number (despite the fact that drones as large as a jet and as tiny as a mosquito have already been produced). Why? After an accident, law enforcement would know whose drone was involved.

That's helpful, but it doesn't hide an uncomfortable reality: Reacting slowly while innovation is occurring quickly is a toxic—if not outright dangerous—combination.

Sony and BlackBerry suffered a similar plight. Despite being reasonably adept at putting out fires left and right, they were unable to survive in this new age of explosive, exponential change. Let's look back at the launch of the first iPhone. When the press asked the CEO of BlackBerry's Research in Motion if the launch of the first iPhone was a threat to his business, he responded by wondering out loud who would ever want to watch video on a phone.

Once the gold standard among technology companies, Research in Motion's stock topped $230 a share in mid-2007. As of December 2016, the stock was hovering around $7.52—not much more than the price of a mediocre pizza.

These are just a few examples that underscore the critical value of anticipatory thinking—the learned competency that allows you to proactively anticipate disruption and change and, from there, plan with the confidence that certainty can provide. That's an ability made all the more essential when you understand that the skills and competencies organizations and companies have traditionally marched in lockstep with are proving increasingly ineffective.

A Dangerous Misconception

This discussion of the ability to anticipate the future highlights a very dangerous misconception. An old expression holds the only two things certain about the future are death and taxes. Phrased another way: Other than those two rather bleak topics, it's impossible to know what the future holds.

I often encounter this sort of skepticism. Even among people who are otherwise open-minded and receptive to ideas outside their usual thinking, there's a prevailing, rather rigid mindset that it's impossible to forecast the future with any accuracy.

To which I respond: "Did you celebrate New Year's this year, and do you know when the next New Year's is coming?" Of course. "Do you know when you have to pay taxes each year?" Yes, and you plan for that certainty. "Can scientists predict the tides and phases of the moon, even years in advance?" They certainly can.

These and other examples underscore an ongoing contradiction—in one breath, we deny that predictability exists, yet we constantly rely on the fact it does. There are literally hundreds of events and occurrences that are, in fact, predictable with the utmost accuracy. If you take a moment, you could probably name dozens of other examples in addition to the ones I just cited. (For the record, there are some 500 known cycles including business, climate, biological, and sales that repeat with utter reliability.)

To assume otherwise is a dangerous misconception—one that limits vision, clouds our perception of possibilities, and, if nothing else, runs counter to our very behavior.

Strategic Foresight and Why People Don't Trust Trends

The world today is riddled with uncertainty at any number of levels—global warming, a volatile global economy, an aging population that may or may not have sufficient funds to retire comfortably. Given that pervasive uncertainty, we all have to ask: "What *can* we be certain about?" The AO Model helps to answer that question, time and again.

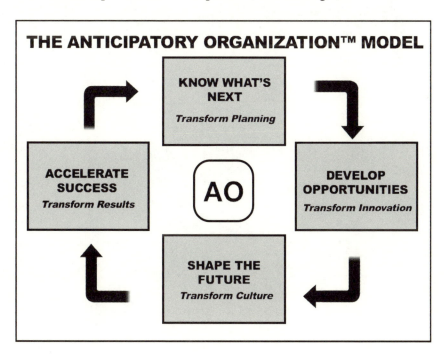

"The AO Model has the power to shift an organization's operating mindset from the default of reacting and responding to changes coming from the outside in, to a place of empowerment by anticipating and shaping the future from the inside out."

The AO Model will allow you to see the future with great accuracy and, from there, make critical decisions and plans with confidence and certainty. It provides a way to drive Exponential Innovation with lower risk through a revolutionary type of trend analysis that will allow you to predict future disruptions, problems, and customer needs, as well as identify game-changing opportunities. The AO Model has the power to shift an organization's operating mindset from the default of reacting and responding to changes coming from the outside in to a place of empowerment by anticipating and shaping the future from the inside out.

This begins with the art of identifying "future facts" and the concept of Hard and Soft Trends.

Chapter 2

Identifying Future Facts— Hard Trends *Will* Happen

We're going to be spending the rest of our lives in the future. Given that reality, why do we spend such little time or energy trying to anticipate what it has in store for us? Contrary to popular opinion, anticipating the future is not an impossible task—provided you know how and where to look—and it all begins with understanding the difference between Hard and Soft Trends.

Hard and Soft Trends are at the core of the AO Model. They are based on more than 30 years of research and analysis. It's strategically important to understand how to recognize Hard and Soft Trends and how to differentiate between the two. Doing so will allow you to forecast the future far more accurately. Moreover, they are critical elements of your ability to accelerate innovation, manage risk at a much higher level, and actively shape the future. If you could accurately predict a big part of the future, would you have a business and personal advantage? I know you would agree the answer is yes!

> **"If you could accurately predict a big part of the future, would you have a business and personal advantage? I know you would agree the answer is yes!"**

Hard Trends

A Hard Trend is a future fact that can provide something that is very empowering: certainty. Hard Trends *will* happen, no matter who you are, whether you're as big as an Apple or a Google, or you're a president or prime minister. None of us can stop Hard Trends from occurring, but there are ways to see them coming.

Hard Trends fall into three primary categories:

- **Technology.** Virtualization, mobility, data analytics, artificial intelligence (AI), the use of the cloud, and social technologies will continue to grow in impact and importance. Genomics will increasingly be used to personalize medicine. These are all examples of Hard Trends that are growing at an exponential rate. None of them represent a temporary fad that will stop being used.

- **Demographics.** There are more than 78 million Baby Boomers in the United States, and they will continue to get older. None of them will get any younger. That's a future certainty—a Hard Trend. And, as they age, there are many predictable problems and opportunities we can be certain about. For example, as they age, a growing number of Baby Boomers will need personalized knee replacements as well as other youth-enhancing treatments to keep them active and feeling young.

- **Government Regulation.** No matter what any politician of any philosophical persuasion might argue, we're going to have more government regulation in the future—not less. And this is true for every country. Increasing regulation around cybersecurity and the use of autonomous vehicles are good examples.

Whenever I deliver a keynote speech on this topic, I collect one Hard Trend certainty and a related opportunity from every audience member. After more than a decade of giving speeches all over the world, I have amassed tens of thousands of Hard Trends and related opportunities—and I can guarantee there are thousands more. (Because all of my audiences are senior-level leaders, think of it as executive-level crowdsourcing on a massive scale.) These Hard Trends will impact every industry, organization, and individual.

Speaking for myself, I utilize Hard Trends to understand what will happen before it happens whenever possible. Let's face it: Those who can't anticipate the future will be forced to react and deal with events as best as they can, falling further behind every year as the pace of change accelerates. And, as history shows, that can lead to very unpleasant outcomes.

However, for those who have learned to anticipate disruptions, problems, and opportunities, there lie enormous untapped opportunities and the ability to shift from reacting to actively shaping the future. By learning how to identify Hard Trends, you can plan with high levels of certainty and can make bold moves with confidence. You can become the disruptor. Using Hard Trends, you can jump ahead of the competition with low risk. Put another way, you can lead without bleeding.

It's important to recognize the distinction between Hard Trends and cyclical change. Like Hard Trends, there are hundreds of cycles that allow you to accurately anticipate the future, including seasonal, economic, and biological cycles. By definition and function, cycles repeat.

Hard Trends can be found by looking at cycles, which most of us understand and use to some degree. But their biggest value comes from learning to identify linear, one-way, and exponential change. Unlike cycles, both linear and exponential changes are one-way and impossible to reverse. Once you've started using a smartphone, there's no way you're going back to a "dumb" phone. Once people in China park their bicycles and get a car, they will not go back to bicycles. On a larger scale, once Baby Boomers hit 65 years of age, they aren't going to turn back the clock and get any younger.

It's beneficial to understand that a Hard Trend can effectively make a form of cyclical change obsolete. Consider the cycle of the production of fruits and vegetables. It used to be said that certain types of fruits and vegetables were "out of season"—tomatoes in the winter, for instance—and, as such, were unavailable. But technology innovations in logistics, like the capacity to move goods from all parts of the world in a matter of hours, has made most forms of produce available year-round. Add to that the trend of vertical farming—produce grown in large buildings with vertically stacked layers—and the same fruits and vegetables that had to be shipped halfway around the world can be grown nearly anywhere. That's an early-stage Hard Trend that makes the once widely accepted cycle of seasonal produce increasingly moot.

It's also valuable to consider your attitude toward Hard Trends. Hard Trends are inevitable, and there's a good chance you may not like some of them. As I mentioned earlier, there will be increasingly more government regulation in the coming years. For many, that's a frustrating, perhaps even maddening, future certainty, as more government oversight means greater constraint, loss of control, and less autonomy.

However, for those who can anticipate the future with an eye toward being the disruptor rather than the disrupted, even what seems to be a problematic Hard Trend can be leveraged to their advantage. As an example, the US government has been requiring the use of electronic patient records from health care providers. That's a Hard Trend, and there's no going back. For many, shifting over to electronic patient records is an expensive, time-intensive activity. But remember, it's not what you do; it's how you do it that will determine an activity's effectiveness. Many e-patient record systems were not implemented with a high level of foresight.

This government regulation created a Hard Trend that provided enormous opportunity for those who took the time to look more closely and take advantage of the billions of dollars the government would pay out to any company, large or small, that could help make this happen. The companies who took that closer look profited handsomely—all from a Hard Trend that merely angered others.

There's an important point about Hard Trends: You can wring your hands in frustration at their inevitability, or you can anticipate and act on their inherent opportunity. What would you rather do?

Here are some additional examples of Hard Trends:

- The increasing use of mobile apps for business areas such as purchasing, supply chain, logistics, customer service, maintenance, and sales support.

- The increasing use of wearables for remote medical diagnostics and chronic disease management.

- In the real estate industry, the increasing use of AI-assisted systems and checklists for processing and closing transactions.

- The exponential growth rate of networked machines and sensors all talking to each other adding intelligence to everything from roads to the paint in hospital rooms.

- The increase in regulations governing the use of drones, autonomous vehicles, and recording wearables.

Soft Trends

Soft Trends are another important component in anticipating and shaping the future. A Soft Trend is a future "maybe," a projection based on statistics and other measures that has the appearance of a tangible, fully predictable fact but is in reality based on assumptions. Therefore, Soft Trends are things that *might* happen.

Here are a few examples of Soft Trends:

- As I write this, global stock markets are in a state of flux, having lost a good deal of their value in recent weeks. A Soft Trend would suggest this is likely to continue in the near future.

But a look back can help put this all into greater perspective. When the housing market collapsed in the early portion of the 21st century, the stock market also suffered a severe drop. The situation was further exacerbated by lenders offering mortgages to buyers with suspect finances. That contributed to the decline in the stock market—it was undeniably steep. It was a tough time, but stocks have since recovered nicely. In fact, we're at record highs. Further, not only have housing prices recovered as well, but some real estate professionals actually took advantage of the decline by focusing their activity on foreclosures. While other real estate offices were closing, some were leveraging difficult conditions and growing. That's a great example of a Soft Trend that you can influence, one that many used to their advantage.

- Obesity has been a rising trend in the United States for well over a decade and is predicted by the US government to continue to grow, becoming a much bigger problem by 2025. However, the rising trend in obesity is a good example of a Soft Trend that can be influenced. It may happen, but it is not a future fact. Understanding this, the government, as well as businesses and individuals, should focus more on how to change this Soft Trend rather than calculating how to underwrite the expense if this Soft Trend is allowed to continue.

- Facebook is the dominant social media platform and is predicted to maintain that position over the next decade. That's a Soft Trend, because any company's dominance depends on leadership and vision. The same holds true for Apple and others—it's a Soft Trend that they will continue in a dominant position. In the late 1990s, Yahoo was the clear leader in the search engine field, but that didn't make their future leadership a fact.

- It will be increasingly difficult to attract and keep talent. This is a Soft Trend, because any company or organization can change this trend by creating an environment where both young and old come together to focus on actively reinventing their industry and creating transformational change.

Remember: Soft trends may seem to be based on reasonably plausible information—and, very often, they do happen—but that doesn't make them a future fact. Because Soft Trends are based on assumptions, there is a greater amount of risk in counting on a Soft Trend to continue. We can assume that Facebook will remain the major player in social media. We can assume that since fewer people have become doctors in the United States over the past decade, that trend will continue. But assuming something is true doesn't push it anywhere closer to an absolute certainty.

It's important to understand that there are two types of assumptions underlying Soft Trends. I call them Hard Assumptions and Soft Assumptions. A Hard Assumption derives from credible data. For example, when looking at the long-term patterns of health care costs, we have compiled statistics and information from the past that suggest that the expense of health care is going to continue to increase in the future. Although that is a Soft Trend—one that can be changed if certain actions are taken—the fact that health care costs have increased steadily in the past, a Hard Assumption, makes it likely that health care will continue to become more expensive. Soft Assumptions lack that underlying, quantifiable form of support and evidence. A Soft Assumption comes from an opinion or some form of gut-level instinct: "I know this new product is going to be a winner!"

If a statement like that makes you uneasy, you have good reason to be. Soft Trends that derive from Soft Assumptions are far less likely to happen than Hard Assumption–driven Soft Trends and pose a much higher level of risk. Planning and decisions based on Soft Trends that start off with a Soft Assumption can get you into a lot of trouble very quickly. For example, when the Affordable Care Act (ACA) was implemented, there

was a Soft Assumption that there would be enough young people sign-
ing up to offset the higher costs of older participants. But there was one
problem: There was no research in place to support that—one of many
Soft Assumptions that had an adverse effect on the ACA's launch.

That naturally raises a question: If Hard Trends are so rock solid
and certain, why bother to pay any attention at all to Soft Trends—
things that may or may not occur?

Personally, I love Soft Trends. Why? Because they are open to influence—meaning you can leverage them to your advantage. Remember in chapter 1 when I discussed the difference between change that
comes from the outside in—a form of change that mandates some
form of reaction—and change that comes from the inside out, which
allows you more control of your future and, from a business perspective, allows you to be the disruptor instead of the disrupted? Soft Trends
are the ideal vehicle for just that sort of change—change that you can
direct and influence, rather than just endure.

Let's return to our Baby Boomer example for a perspective on how
this can work. The fact that Baby Boomers are all getting older is a
Hard Trend. Naturally, many of them will retire, taking with them
years of experience, insight, and wisdom. A Soft Trend would be that
as Baby Boomers continue to retire by the thousands, they take their
valuable experience with them. How can you influence this Soft Trend?
What if you implemented a system through which you could collect
and organize all that valuable knowledge and wisdom beforehand and
put it on a knowledge-sharing network? That's an ideal example of a
Soft Trend that you could actually influence.

When properly identified, Soft Trends can be leveraged and influenced to unlock enormous opportunity. That becomes all the more
so when a Soft Trend is supported by a Hard Assumption, such as the
number of Baby Boomers who are retiring. This affords greater certainty and confidence in acting to use the Soft Trend to your advantage.

As we did with Hard Trends, let's pose a few additional examples
of Soft Trends:

- An increasing number of American homes will house multigenerational families.

- Internationally, China's demand for raw materials will never decline.

- No European nation will ever go so far financially as to fall into default.

- Tesla will continue to be the leader in manufacturing high-end, American-made electronic vehicles.

- Bitcoin will continue to be the dominant cybercurrency.

Separating Hard Trends from Soft Trends

Implicit in our discussion of various types of trends is the challenge of telling them apart from one another. Don't worry; it's not as difficult as it might seem. But it is critical to identifying the enormous game-changing opportunities that an anticipatory competency can uncover.

What if you find yourself debating if a trend is hard or soft? Here's a simple guide that can help: If you're taking some time to decide whether a trend is hard or soft, it's a Soft Trend. As a rule, Hard Trends are sufficiently evident—like the increasing need for cybersecurity, the increasing use of cloud services, and Baby Boomers growing older—and thus naturally and quickly separate themselves from Soft Trends.

Since mistaking a Soft Trend for a Hard Trend can be a costly misstep, the distinction between the two is important to recognize. In speaking to various groups, I regularly cite several examples of Soft Trends that were assumed to be Hard Trends. Exhaustive strategies and billions of dollars were built around the assumption that these trends were Hard Trends when they actually turned out to be Soft Trends. Here are a few with which you're likely familiar:

- Home prices will never go down.

- Saudi Arabia will never let the price of oil crash.

- The largest financial institutions in the world
  will never fail.

You can appreciate the consequences of treating these and other examples like them as though they were future facts. None of them were, in fact, absolute certainties—and those who believed otherwise were grossly mistaken.

But the fact that a trend is a Soft Trend rather than Hard Trend isn't a problem in the least (but mistaking one for the other is!). As I've pointed out, I love Soft Trends because they're open to change.

Nor is one trend—Hard or Soft—necessarily more important than the other. Both can be used to your advantage. It all depends on recognizing what is a Hard Trend and what is a Soft Trend, whether Soft Trends are based on a Hard Assumption or a Soft Assumption, and the interplay between them. Taken together, they can all be leveraged to unlock enormous opportunity.

NAME THAT TREND . . .

Identifying whether a trend is Hard or Soft—as well as other characteristics—is a central component of the AO Model. Here's a short quiz to help you improve your skills in this important area.

Directions: In the example below, you'll find a trend or development of some sort. Your first challenge, based on the guidelines you've read about in this chapter, is to determine whether that trend is a Hard Trend or Soft Trend. If it's a Soft Trend, you'll be charged with identifying whether it has an underlying Hard Assumption or Soft Assumption. Your next question is whether that trend is cyclical (cycles repeat like seasons or the stock market) linear (growing in one direction), or exponential (something that is one-way and doubling in speed as it transforms over time).

The purpose of this exercise is to help hone your ability to identify critical elements related to anticipating the future. The differences are important. To recap, Hard Trends are based on a future fact: They *will* happen. Soft Trends are based on assumptions, and they might happen. If a Soft Trend is based on a Hard Assumption—the underlying assumption was well researched—it is more likely to happen. If it was based on a Soft Assumption—the underlying assumption made sense, or you used a "gut" feeling—it is less likely to happen. Linear change is one-way, as is exponential change. The key difference is that exponential change continually gathers momentum and speed by doubling and, as a result, can lead to outright transformation.

Here's an example to get you started:

Example	Type of Trend	Type of Assumption	Type of Change
	Hard Trend or Soft Trend	Hard Assumption or Soft Assumption	Cyclical Linear Exponential
Baby Boomers retiring	Hard Trend	N/A	Linear

Got the hang of it? Here are some other examples for you to work on (answers are keyed below).

To further the value of this exercise, use this as a worksheet as you gain skill in the AO Model. Identify your own trends and from there, break them down into Hard Trends and Soft Trends (and, as necessary, Hard and Soft Assumptions) as well as cyclical, linear, or exponential change. The more you practice, the more your ability to effectively anticipate the future will improve—as will your ability to plan with greater confidence and lower risk.

Quiz	Type of Trend	Type of Assumption	Type of Change
	Hard Trend or Soft Trend	Hard Assumption or Soft Assumption	Cyclical Linear Exponential
1. Increasing industry convergence			
2. Increasing use of social media			
3. Increasing obesity			
4. Increasing use of mobile technology			
5. Increasing difficulty in attracting talent			

Answers: 1. Increasing industry convergence: Hard Trend, N/A, Exponential **2.** Increasing use of social media: Hard Trend, N/A, Exponential **3.** Increasing obesity: Soft Trend, Hard Assumption, N/A **4.** Increasing use of mobile technology, N/A, Exponential **5.** Increasing difficulty in attracting talent: Soft Trend, Hard Assumption, N/A

Here's an ideal example. Recently, I was speaking to the presidents of a number of colleges and universities. They were all looking at their demographics, worried about decreasing student numbers, particularly at the smaller schools. How, they asked me, can we boost our enrollment? How can we differentiate ourselves from other schools?

I suggested we first look at some Hard Trends. As our dependence on technology is growing, cybersecurity becomes increasingly important—a solid Hard Trend that has both threats and opportunities. Couple that with the Soft Trend of decreasing college enrollment—a distressing Soft Trend, to be sure, but a Soft Trend that's open to change and influence.

So, I suggested to them, "What if you established a degree program in cybersecurity and data forensics? What if you did a good job building that program, attracting top-notch faculty, and offering a cutting-edge curriculum? Do you think you'd have people from all over the country wanting to come to your school?"

Of course, every one of them agreed enthusiastically! So I took things a few steps further: "How about courses in data analytics? How about 3D printing? How about social business enterprise management? How about advanced manufacturing and automation?"

The answer was obvious. Instead of decreasing enrollments, all those schools would have students pounding on their doors begging to enroll in those courses.

At this point, you may be saying: Okay, I get that Hard Trends and Soft Trends can not only help anticipate the future but, more importantly, can be used to shape the future in a positive way. I can also appreciate how valuable that ability could be in identifying fantastic opportunities as I create solid plans with greater confidence and certainty.

But you might also be thinking that it's going to take a great deal of time before these changes and disruptions occur. To help you understand the accelerating time frame, look back at some of the relatively recent technological breakthroughs we have all experienced, such as the switch to flat-panel televisions and the widespread use of cell phones.

It took many years before these became commonplace and really impacted society as a whole.

I hear this from a great many people and can certainly understand that point of view. But that's a view of the future based on past events—the reasoning being that since something occurred at such and such a speed in the past, it's reasonable to expect that it will occur at the same speed in the future.

It may seem reasonable, but it's a mistaken conclusion. The fact is that change is taking place in shorter and shorter amounts of time. Moreover, rather than slowing down or maintaining that pace, change in the future is going to occur at increasingly faster rates of speed—in fact, at an exponential rate of change. That has a great deal to do with the Three Digital Accelerators, which will be one of the focal points of the next chapter.

Transformation will continue to happen at increasingly faster rates of speed. Disruptions will also happen at a faster rate. That raises an essential question: How are you going to deal with that?

Chapter 3

Three Digital Accelerators and the Exponential Inflection Point

Imagine posing this question to your smartphone: "Siri, are we in a period of true transformation?"

That's a very important question, but approach it beyond the parameters of a simple query. For instance, consider that you can actually ask that question of a device that you can hold in your hand as you walk down the street. Consider that the answer to those sorts of questions and queries are coming through your phone's link to a powerful supercomputer in the cloud.

Now, consider how long ago it was that such an everyday activity was relegated to the realm of absolute fantasy.

That illustrates a powerful reality. We are now in the heart of an important time in history. We are doing things today that were impossible just a few years ago. And, given the Hard Trends that are shaping the future, we will be doing things in two years that are impossible today. We have moved from rapid change to outright transformation, from something being merely possible to being a game changer. The fact that you can ask a supercomputer a question while standing at the corner of Fifth and Main is powerful evidence of that truth.

While some of us are very much aware of this reality, as well as its future implications, many are not. In order to effectively direct your organization into the future with confidence and certainty as a leader, it is essential that you recognize it and embrace it—that, and the fact that change and transformation are going to occur far more rapidly than you might even expect.

How we move into the future won't be driven by the same forces that got us here. But that really doesn't matter. We have already reached what could be called an Exponential Inflection Point—a point that marks a shift in the forces that will drive exponential growth and transformation at increasingly faster and faster rates of speed.

How We Got Here

Understanding how we got to this point—and how we're going to keep moving forward with exponential growth and transformation—begins with understanding the predictable impact and scope of the Three Digital Accelerators. I first identified them 30 years ago and have since used them to make hundreds of accurate predictions and forecasts in computing, communication, genomics, material science, medical device development, and many more areas.

The Three Digital Accelerators are:

1. **Computing Power.** For the past five decades, this was tied to the predictable, exponential growth in processing power and the decreasing price of integrated circuits—summarized for the past 50 years by Moore's Law. Today and beyond, exponential growth has shifted to the supercomputing power we access in the cloud, where it continues to grow at an exponential rate (a subject I'll get to shortly).

2. **Bandwidth.** The capacity of digital networks and our electronic communication systems to transfer data has experienced predictable, exponential growth while the cost has decreased at a similar rate.

3. **Digital Storage.** The method used to store, maintain, manage, and back up data has—like bandwidth—experienced predictable, exponential increases in capacity while the price has gone down at a similar rate.

In 1983, I was the first to identify the power of combining all Three Digital Accelerators—computing power in conjunction with bandwidth and digital storage—and link them as an exponential driver of economic value creation for decades to come. It's been an enormously powerful trifecta that has proven itself over time.

The Exponential Inflection Point—It's What You Can Do, Not Just How Fast

One of the primary targets of those who believe the rate of exponential change we've experienced can't possibly continue has been Moore's Law (for more details about Moore's Law, refer to page 33). In fact, predictions about the demise of Moore's Law have circulated for years. For some, the "cause" is purely technical—there are physical limits to the size of a transistor, they say. Others cite economics. The cost of building manufacturing facilities is already in the billions and going up. The chips they produce simply can't keep getting less expensive as Moore's Law outlines.

MOORE'S LAW

For those of you who may have lost track of Moore's Law, here's a quick overview.

The law is named after Gordon E. Moore, cofounder of Intel and Fairchild Semiconductor. Moore's Law deals with processing power, the speed at which a machine can perform a particular task. In 1965, Moore published a paper in which he observed that between 1958 and 1965 the number of transistors on an integrated circuit had doubled every 18 to 24 months. At the same time, Moore noted, the price of those integrated circuits dropped by half.

Moore projected this would continue for some time but did not say for how long. (The concept has held true for more than 50 years.)

Here's an example of Moore's Law in exponential action. In 1958, a scientist at Texas Instruments developed the first integrated circuit. It contained two transistors with a gate process length of roughly one-half inch.

In 1971, Moore's company, Intel, debuted its first commercial product, a 4-bit CPU called the Intel 4004 integrated circuit. The 4004 had 2,300 transistors with a gate length of 10,000 nanometers and a computing power of about 740 KHz. The average cost of a transistor at the time: $1.

Let's jump ahead roughly 40 years. In 2012, Nvidia released a new graphical processor unit (GPU) with 7.1 billion transistors, a gate length of 28 nanometers, and processing power of 7GHz. Average cost of a transistor: approximately $0.0000001.

In the past 40 years, the technology experienced a 100 billion-fold improvement in performance and a concomitant drop in price, right on schedule per Moore's Law—although, as we discuss in this chapter, some are worried that Moore's Law no longer holds true and that, consequently, technological innovation and advances will slow considerably. In 2017, Intel once again showed that Moore's Law is alive and well with another innovation in chip design, but, as you'll see, exponential growth is expanding beyond individual chips.

Not only has that led many to believe that advances in technology are going to come at a slower pace than they have up to this point, it's also lulled them into a false sense of security and even complacency: "Well, since things are slowing down because Moore's Law no longer applies, I'll have more time to react to those new forms of digital disruption that might show up."

To which I reply: Never underestimate the inventive creativity of engineers who love doing the impossible, and Moore's Law is tied to the power of the chips in our devices. We're less dependent on the exponentially growing power of these chips today, because we are using our devices to tap into supercomputers in the cloud. The continued exponential growth of the capabilities of the overall computing ecosystem of which the chips in our devices, the bandwidth we use to access everything, and the digital storage we rely on is merely one part. The most advanced supercomputers and artificial intelligence are now helping us design the next generation supercomputer that will keep the exponential growth of the ecosystem growing. It's important to understand that we have reached an Exponential Inflection Point on the exponential curve, because the rate of change is beginning to appear to be going utterly vertical.

This also undermines the idea that we'll all have more time to understand and embrace technological change. In fact, the very reverse is true. Given the speed of change afforded by the Exponential Tipping Point, things are going to be happening faster and faster. Time is very much on the side of digital transformation; not your ability to react to it.

Here's some perspective. Not very long ago, a laptop was largely a stand-alone device. Its functions and capabilities were internally focused—the computer's storage and processing power derived solely from its internal chips. How it worked depended exclusively on whatever was inside.

Not anymore. For one thing, we now use a smartphone or tablet to perform many of the functions our laptops used to. Thanks to tools such as Apple's Siri and Google Now, combined with greater bandwidth, any one of us can now tap into the capabilities of the world's supercomputers with just a few spoken words. With the cloud, our storage capability is no longer limited to what any one device can store internally.

Looked at another way, you have the computing power of the world in your pocket, and it isn't solely because of the chips inside a device. Nor is it just a matter of processing power. What matters now is overall computing power—all the things you're capable of doing that you couldn't do a very short time ago. So, from this point forward, it's more appropriate to think of overall computing power rather than just processing power.

Here's yet another way to look at this. Daniel Reed, a computer scientist at the University of Iowa, once pointed out a comparison between a Boeing 707 of the 1970s versus the Boeing 787 of today. If all you're focused on is speed, there isn't much to occupy your attention, as the Boeing 787 doesn't fly all that much faster than its earlier counterpart. What really matters are the other aspects of the newer aircraft. The 787 is far more fuel efficient than the 707. It pollutes less and has a lighter, more air-efficient frame that makes the 707 look almost primitive. Some say this innovation, along with others in overall noise level and stability, may make jet lag and air sickness things of the past.

No, it's not all that much faster than its counterpart that's some 60 years old, but so what? It's all the other things that the aircraft can do that make it transformative.

That also applies to tools you use on a daily basis, such as a smartphone, tablet, laptop, or desktop. Consider the following:

- If the tools mentioned above were 100 times as powerful and less expensive, what could you do professionally that you cannot do now?

- If your Internet connection was 100 times as fast as it is now, what type of high-value services could you provide that would be impossible today?

- If you could store 100 times as much data at half the cost, how would this impact your business processes?

- If your customers could enjoy all of the benefits mentioned above, would that change their businesses?

Nor is this Exponential Inflection Point limited to advances in technology. Competitive barriers have fallen as the result of the growing power of the devices we use. Thanks to resources readily available on the Internet and elsewhere, you can easily build your own app. If money's an issue, use Kickstarter to raise capital. New resources have opened up enormous opportunities in every marketplace that in the past were limited to large companies or people with significant financial resources and manpower. That's a form of outright transformation, and one not measured solely by technological advances.

The transformation we're experiencing now and will experience in the future is particularly striking when charted on a graph. At the beginning, the level of change was relatively flat. But as it grew, it began to curve upwards—something like the blade of a hockey stick. Now, the blade has shifted into a completely vertical angle. That's exponential, rapid change that is, in fact, transformation.

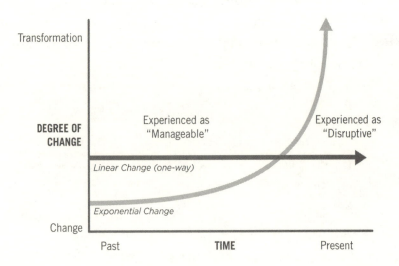

If you're still concerned that Moore's Law is slipping away, relax. For one thing, chip development is no longer focused on computational "brute strength." It's more specialized, meaning that overall computing power will continue to improve as supercomputers design faster supercomputers, and AI is distributed via the cloud. (Again, the overall ecosystem is more important than any one part.) And, as these and other advances drive transformation, they'll also devise new ways to move forward with chip development and other technologies—only in a different way than we saw in years past.

All this unlocks enormous opportunity for those who are aware of the speed with which every element of our lives is being transformed. As a leader, understanding that computing power is not merely an issue of speed but of what can be accomplished by new and powerful tools, not only broadens your thinking as to how these tools may be used to your best advantage, but it also confirms that new and innovative technology has no intention of slowing down—it's only going to become faster, and exponentially so.

The Interplay Between Possible, Useful, and Exceptional

At this point, it's valuable to consider the nuance between when a particular form of technology, product, or service is truly exceptional, and when it's merely useful or even possible. This shifts the discussion to the issue of when change and innovation can be used to your best advantage.

For instance, when Siri was introduced, it was far from optimal. Sure, it was cool to use and foreshadowed what it would be able to do in time, but it was anything but an exceptional user experience. Why? The Three Digital Accelerators had not been developed to the point to make the experience optimal.

You've seen it firsthand yourself. Back in 2000, your Wi-Fi was deadly slow, if you had it at all. But it was

> **"All this unlocks enormous opportunity for those who are aware of the speed with which every element of our lives is being transformed. "**

there, and if you had it, you used it nevertheless. Again, though, the experience was anything but outstanding.

Why didn't Apple release the iPhone two years earlier? They could have produced it, but the experience would have been terrible. The video would have been awful. Why didn't Netflix start with streaming video? The Three Digital Accelerators were not ready to deliver a good customer experience yet. Instead, they started with a postal revolution, creating a mailer in which you received your DVD and then used later to mail the DVD back whenever you wanted. Thanks to barcodes on the mailers, Netflix knew that the old DVD was back and they could send you the next one you requested. The idea of going to a Block-buster store to rent a movie was rendered utterly obsolete—as were, not to mention everyone's favorite topic, late fees!

Think of it as three points: possible, useful, and optimal. It used to take a long time to get to possible, and subsequently, to get from possible to useful. This process is being compressed into shorter and shorter amounts of time because of where we are now along the exponential curve of the Three Digital Accelerators, as well as the additional factors that make up the overall ecosystem we discussed earlier—pricing, competition, and others.

In some cases, it makes sense to introduce a new product or service whose performance—since the Three Digital Accelerators don't yet support it—is less than optimal. Get your foot in the door and offer something that people will find cool and engaging but will also be willing to wait for until it can become truly exceptional. In others, it's better to hold off until the Digital Accelerators allow for a fantastic, superior experience.

Take that into account when considering how the predictable acceleration of computing power, bandwidth, and digital storage can best be used in your organization or professional life. For instance, say you're a real estate agent who would like to post virtual home tours with augmented reality on your website. Do your clients have sufficient bandwidth to give them a great experience or would it be smarter to hold off until adequate bandwidth ensures optimal service? No matter your organization, is it built on the quality of customer and user experience, or is it more at home with experimentation?

To See the Future More Accurately Think Both/And—Not Either/Or

All this change and transformation can be very exciting. And it's very easy to get caught up in the fervor when new technology or products are introduced. Just look at the lines of people camping outside an Apple store days in advance of the release of a new iPhone as evidence of the sort of interest and anticipation these developments can generate.

In fact, that level of excitement can go a bit overboard—not so much in terms of spending days shivering in a sleeping bag outside a storefront, but in how we approach the new technology relative to the technology that preceded it.

Whenever new technology is introduced, we tend to think it mandates an absolute choice between the old or the new. Executives, management, and the media feed into that either/or mindset—either we do this, or we do that; it's either the old or the new. In effect, the question becomes whether you fully embrace the future or prefer to protect the past. It's one or the other, and there is no middle ground.

Further, we all assume that the introduction of new technology is a death knell for whatever preceded it. We think the new version must be so much better in every way imaginable that the older device or technology will simply dry up, blow away, and cease to exist. But that's seldom the way it works. And it's valuable to understand why.

However new and improved, the hottest breakthrough technologies don't necessarily replace the old ones. Instead, they often coexist side by side for quite some time. Think about it: We have digital media all over the place, but print newspapers and magazines still exist. We have digital, downloadable music, but you still see CDs everywhere you look. We still use credit cards even though our smartphone-enabled payment is much more secure.

Older technology often has its own unique profile of functional strengths that the new technology can never fully replace. Phrased another way: It's not an either/or world we live in. It's a both/and world.

> "From now on, when a new technology comes out, instead of assuming a choice between old or new, consider instead how you can integrate the old with the new to create higher value than either would have on their own."

And the key to success is to understand that it's the integration of the old with the new that creates greater value than either would have on their own.

For example, mainframe computers might seem as outdated as black-and-white televisions and eight-track tapes. But are we still using them? Yes, only in a different manner than we did 10, 20, or 30 years ago. Our go-to personal computer is most often our smartphone or tablet—yet we still have laptops and desktop computers. We may be using them less than we did in the past and in different ways. But they're still there, and we're still using them.

That underscores an important idea. From now on, when a new technology comes out, instead of assuming a choice between old or new, consider instead how you can integrate the old with the new to create higher value than either would have on their own. The key, the real magic of both old and new, is integration: direct mail and email, old media and new media, voice and data, full service and self-service. By balancing the two, you give each more value than they would have individually.

It's clear that we're in a unique period of transformation, one that we've never experienced before. That calls for transformational thinking—if you're merely changing or tweaking a product, service, or process, you're likely to fall behind. It's usually impossible to quickly dump older legacy systems and rapidly switch to the new—but by focusing on integrating the old with the new to create greater value during the migration, organizations can more fully leverage the opportunity that these sorts of rapid transitions afford us.

DEVELOP OPPORTUNITIES— *TRANSFORM INNOVATION*

Chapter 4

Radically Accelerate Innovation

As I pointed out in chapter 1, we are standing at the base of a mountain of disruption and change, that's filled with problems and transformational opportunities as well as the ability to innovate at levels mankind has never before experienced. The speed at which we are all approaching the mountain is increasing at an exponential rate, and the mountain is steep. That means good navigation is a must.

For the vast majority of us, the mountain that lies ahead is shrouded in fog, making it not only hard to navigate but easy to take the wrong turn or hit unforeseen obstacles that pop up out of nowhere. But those who have the tools to cut through the fog, and the desire to shape a positive future by driving innovation, can turn disruption and change into opportunity and advantage.

Most companies only pursue innovation incrementally because of the risks involved. Given the danger and expense, they're very cautious about doing anything too big and bold. But organizations that understand Hard Trend and Soft Trend methodologies see that the risk of not innovating is actually greater than the risk of innovating. As a result, they can use these methodologies to find new ways to navigate the mountain and manage the risks associated with innovation. Knowing the Hard Trend certainties that will happen in the future, as well as things that may happen but are open to influence, allow companies to innovate far faster, jumping ahead with much lower risk. They have the confidence to make bold moves. They have the confidence to both navigate and climb that mountain of opportunity at a much faster rate than others.

There's certainly no lack of books, strategies, and other materials that address innovation. Not only does the AO Model detail how organizations can innovate with far lower risk and greater success, it also identifies two very different forms of innovation that are commonly overlooked but can have great impact.

The first is Everyday Innovation. This is the kind of innovation that anyone at any level within an organization can perform on a daily basis to devise inventive solutions to everyday problems.

The second is Exponential Innovation. This is game-changing, disruptive innovation—the kind that can upend an entire industry but, as I'll explain, can still be pursued with low risk and greater confidence than that of innovators who do not know how to identify the forces that are shaping the future.

By learning to implement these two types of transformative innovation, you have the opportunity to radically accelerate innovation throughout your organization. While others settle for slogging along with slow, incremental innovation, you can leap far ahead by using the Hard Trends that are shaping the future to craft bold decisions that derive from confidence.

And, as you'll see, the first step is keeping your antenna up, all the time.

No Antenna, Nothing to See

Recently, I was chatting with a young man who graduated with a business degree and was working for a driving instruction company. The topic of driverless cars came up. I asked him if they might put his company out of business.

My young friend shrugged. "That won't matter for a long, long time," he replied.

As you're reading this, you're probably aware of the growing number of semiautonomous and even fully autonomous cars that are now on the road. This intelligent young man knew all about driverless cars, but he was not connecting them to his work.

Why? He didn't have his antenna up.

Here's what I mean by that. All of us routinely read or hear about some extraordinary new technology, product, or breakthrough. How do we often react? We say, "Wow, that's really something," and then go back to being busy, hunkering down to business as usual. The issues of the moment are our sole concern.

Someone whose antenna is up reacts very differently. Instead of quickly getting back to what she may have been doing, she begins to ask questions. How might this affect me, now and in the future? Does this correlate to any new, disruptive Hard or Soft Trend? Can it offer any sort of advantage?

When your antenna is up, you're tuned into new opportunities to innovate that others fail to see. You're focused on the future and how you can impact it, rather than just waiting to be surprised. That's why this level of awareness is the first step toward radical innovation.

My young friend shouldn't feel badly. He has a lot of company. Consider Dell, Sony, HP, BlackBerry, Blockbuster, Kodak, and countless other organizations. It's safe to say their antennas weren't up. As a result, they couldn't see the game-changing innovations that were happening all around them.

I have seen this disconnect countless times at the highest executive levels. It's not a form of denial—as human beings, we all have a tendency to slip back into an embrace of the status quo, no matter how obvious coming change might be. But the disconnect is more dangerous than many of us might think.

The Dangers of Rearview Mirror Thinking

Another way to frame this discussion is by what I refer to as Rearview Mirror Thinking. This is an important concept to understand, as it's central to moving toward an Anticipatory Mindset. Rearview Mirror Thinking is the tendency to use your past experience as a means of framing the future—in other words, using past precedent as your primary reference point as you look forward.

Let's revisit an example I cited in chapter 1 with this concept in mind. When the iPhone was introduced, reporters asked the CEO of BlackBerry—then the dominant player in the business mobile phone field—if he saw a threat to his business. He replied, in effect, that he couldn't see why anyone would want to watch video on a phone. In making that remark, the executive was using a combination of current and Rearview Mirror Thinking. Since no one had ever devised a phone capable of playing video, he couldn't imagine its appeal on such a small screen. How inaccurate his perception proved to be!

In the young man's case I mentioned earlier, his Rearview Mirror Thinking of the future told him that since an innovation as disruptive as driverless cars was so massive, it would likely take a decade or even longer to impact his business. Rearview Mirror Thinking is also very either/or in nature. In this example, it was either a matter of cars remaining as they are now or becoming completely driverless.

Will young people still need to learn how to drive? Of course. Can you picture Porsche selling a car without a steering wheel? Not likely. Because we like to drive—what we don't like are accidents. But young people won't be learning how to drive in the way they've traditionally been taught. A different kind of driver's education will be needed, and there will likely be less of it. That may mean fewer drivers education instructors, who will require different forms of training themselves.

> "The AO Model is built to enable and instill innovation and transformation on an organization-wide level— and, in so doing, encourage everyone to keep their antennas up at all times."

There's an important lesson in this. As we've discussed, the impact of disruptive innovation is no longer slow. It's growing faster and faster all the time thanks to the exponential speed of the Three Digital Accelerators and the Exponential Inflection Point. To remain leaders in their field, organizations and companies of all sorts have to make innovation an ongoing and encompassing focus.

Hard and Soft Trends, the Three Digital Accelerators, and the Exponential Inflection Point are transforming how we live, work, and play at a pace that the world has never experienced before. Now more than ever, innovation with a focus on transformation is an absolute imperative. As we'll see, the AO Model is built to enable and instill innovation and transformation on an organization-wide level—and, in so doing, encourage everyone to keep their antennas up at all times.

Without that, you're not going to be climbing any mountains any time soon.

Organizations, Not Individuals

Let's take a look at how people and organizations have traditionally viewed innovation.

For some, this word calls to mind a picture of a solitary figure on a mountaintop wrapped in a blanket and engrossed in deep, meditative contemplation, a mystical figure whose sole charge is to unwrap that ethereal mystery that we refer to as innovation—new, different, and powerful ways of thinking and doing things. Others might imagine a person wearing a lab coat, staring intently at a computer deep in some hidden laboratory.

These images are exaggerations, but the characterization is not that far off. In many companies and organizations, innovation has traditionally been left to "them" or "someone else"—some other person or group empowered to identify and implement innovation wherever and whenever they saw fit. Innovation also occurred slowly—change of any sort needed a lot of time. In fact, innovation was, in reality, discouraged in many industries because executing current strategy was the main focus. The risks associated with innovation were seen as a negative. Stick your neck out, and you get it chopped off! Better to simply stay the course.

If, by chance, you worked for a company that *thought* they wanted to innovate, there was either a paper-based or digital equivalent of the good old suggestion box. But—as was the case in one Fortune 100 company with which I worked—the suggestion box became over-stuffed with ideas, and no one had the time to look at all of them. As a result, nothing happened, and people stopped taking the time to offer suggestions. Worse yet, the best and the brightest employees started leaving in search of a better future. This company's revenue and stock price have continued to decline.

In another instance, I worked with a company whose global market dominance was being challenged. The CEO took great pride in asserting how innovative the company was, but when I looked at their products and services, it was clear that they hadn't done anything truly innovative in more than 10 years. Instead, they'd been milking innovations that were upwards of 15 years old, which was why their margins were shrinking. Because they were using Rearview Mirror Thinking when they talked about corporate culture and values, they thought they were an innovative company when they really weren't at all.

The rate of change and transformation we are all experiencing makes innovation—both Everyday as well as Exponential—absolutely essential. Defer to a rearview mirror view of innovation being the responsibility of only certain people and something less than an absolute priority, and you risk falling further and further behind, or worse. Innovation is now everyone's business. The AO Model builds a mindset where innovation can occur all the time and at every level of a company or organization.

> "Innovation is now everyone's business. The AO Model builds a mindset where innovation can occur all the time and at every level of a company or organization."

The Skeptic in the Group

What I am implying in this discussion is that everyone within a company or group embrace an Anticipatory Mindset.

Consider the growing momentum and speed with which technology and other factors are transforming everything we do, both personally as well as professionally. Given the increasing rate of widespread change, it's not difficult to understand that entire companies and organizations—not just certain departments or areas of operation—will be transformed.

Now, assume for a moment that one individual or group refuses to believe—for whatever reason—that transformational change will continue to occur. Moreover, having an Anticipatory Mindset seems impossible to them—in their eyes, not one of us can anticipate the future with any degree of certainty.

It's important to respect their opinion, no matter how much you may disagree. But no matter who that person or group happens to be or what they do, they're bound to have an impact on the overall company or organization's confidence and momentum in effectively anticipating the future, and, as a result, they could act as a brake that slows the pace of innovation. Naturally, the effects may be more pronounced if a company president or head of an organization refuses to consider the value of anticipatory thinking and a broad focus on innovation. But anyone, be they in sales, development, finance, or any other area, can hinder the entire group.

Happily, it's not an unsolvable issue. For one thing, having a skeptic in the group in no way precludes you from using anticipatory thinking and innovation yourself. Yes, there may be a list of certain things you may need approval for from someone else, but there are many things that are a good deal more autonomous. If it helps, draw up a list of all the things you can do completely of your own accord. If it can be done, and you can do it, go ahead and do it!

Also, talk with others who are onboard with anticipatory thinking. Perhaps you can work together to pre-solve a predictable problem or address an opportunity to innovate that goes beyond just one person.

Lastly, arm yourself with the power of persuasion. In chapters 8 and 9, we'll discuss practical strategies for selling your ideas, whether they're going up the chain or moving down. For instance, one of the concepts you'll learn is what I refer to as a "Time Travel Audit," in which you gain a sense of someone's attitude and mindset with regard to the past, present, and future. As you'll learn, some people are more focused on the future, which, naturally enough, makes them more receptive to anticipatory thinking. Others who like to think of the "good old days" are more oriented toward the past. If that's the case, I'll show how you can gently and persuasively walk them into the future.

Performing a Time Travel Audit of your colleagues, your customers, and your organization can dramatically increase the ability to sell your ideas and influence others—and, in doing so, can help persuade the skeptics among you to embrace the value of anticipatory thinking with a focus on driving innovation.

If everyone you work with understands the value of anticipatory thinking and innovation, so much the better. But, even if just one person gets it, there are tools at hand that you can use to actively shape the future.

"I Don't Do Innovation"

"My job isn't innovation." Stop for a moment and think of how many people in your organization would say something just like that.

Again, it's easy to understand how this sort of mindset can take hold. Someone may be perfectly competent at their job—be that as a receptionist, salesperson, engineer, manager, or in any number of other capacities—but their approach to what they do is hindered by tunnel vision. I greet visitors. I take orders over the phone. I raise funds. I examine the company's employment practices to make sure they're in compliance with federal regulations. Put another way: I do what my job description tells me to do. And that doesn't involve innovation. "We have people who do that."

An Anticipatory Organization doesn't promote that fragmented sort of thinking. Rather, it encourages people at all levels of a company or organization to employ anticipatory thinking—and from there, to build a culture of innovation in which everyone can participate, rather than just a select few.

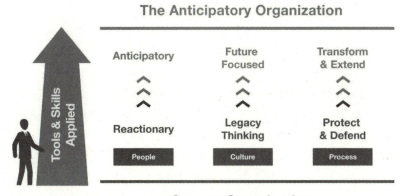

Here are examples of how to use anticipatory thinking for both Everyday and Exponential Innovation. Let's say you work in the sales division of a company. Thinking in an anticipatory manner, what are some of the predictable objections you'll undoubtedly hear from prospects? One of them is probably going to be price. Everybody objects to price. Nobody ever wants something to cost more than they think it should. Everybody wants a deal. We all know someone who constantly brags about all the great deals he got!

If price is an anticipated stumbling block, you can then pre-solve it before it becomes a major issue that discourages sales. If a client raises the question of price, you will already have thought through how to counter with insights about how a particular product can be used to solve multiple problems, thus creating greater value. That justifies a greater cost in the eyes of the customer. Or, maybe you step back and point out that the product they were originally looking for would not solve the underlying "real" problem they had. By offering them a solution to their real problem, you create consultative value that is worth the additional price. Maybe you point out that the most "expensive" choice of all is saying no—one that could imperil the very life of their business. All of these ideas represent Everyday Innovation—using anticipatory thinking to solve predictable problems with an inventive solution on an ongoing, daily basis.

But what about Exponential Innovation? Let's think back to my young friend and the impact of driverless cars. Since he didn't have his antenna up, he didn't see anything beyond what he assumed (incorrectly) was a long time frame. Further, he made no connection to his current job. Now consider the opportunity for Exponential Innovation that's there for him to both see and act on. With the rapid growth of both semiautonomous and fully autonomous vehicles, there is a major opportunity to redefine and reinvent drivers education. By looking at the bigger picture and asking questions such as how this change will affect mass transit, fire and rescue, postal delivery, and even school buses, opportunities to train the people that will be directly controlling or interfacing with these types of vehicles begin to appear.

This is a perfect example of Exponential Innovation: Thinking that was previously focused on teaching young people how to drive has instantaneously blossomed into any number of major opportunities to provide a different type of training for operators and drivers of these vehicles.

Exponential Innovation can occur no matter the setting or circumstances. Let's apply this to foreseeable problems. Going back to my hypothetical example of working in sales, let's say you visit all sorts of companies and organizations. One of them happens to be a hospital. During your sales call, because you have your antenna up and are looking for new opportunities to add consultative value, you hear hospital staff complain that equipment they rely on every day isn't saving them time. The systems are slow and cumbersome and are proving to be increasingly inadequate to handle growing workloads. It's not a real problem yet, but it's getting there quickly.

One way to approach these sorts of foreseeable problems is identifying one or more of what I have defined as the Eight Hard Trend Pathways to Innovation. These represent eight technology Hard Trends that are growing at an exponential rate and can be used to both see and act on new opportunities to drive both Everyday and Exponential Innovation. I'll cover them all in more detail shortly, but, in the meantime, let's examine how two Hard Trend Pathways—dematerialization and virtualization—apply to the hospital scenario I just described.

First, some definitions are in order. Dematerialization means making things smaller—a Hard Trend we have witnessed in our products for decades, from computers to televisions to cellular phones. What is different today is that we have new tools and processes that make dematerialization much easier and faster to accomplish. By asking ourselves what would have far greater value if it were smaller in size, we can see new opportunities to innovate.

Virtualization means taking things we currently do in the physical world and shifting the medium so that we can do them in a digital, weightless, representational world. By asking what physical assets we could virtualize to both lower costs and increase value, or what virtual services we could provide that would create new income streams, we can identify even more opportunities to innovate.

Now let's apply those two Hard Trend Pathways to our example. You might suggest to hospital executives that they look at virtualization and ask themselves if it could be used to address issues proactively before they become problems, such as increasing patient loads and the exponential growth of data. You might suggest using a combination of data analytics and dematerialization—in this case, artificial intelligence—to uncover actionable insights from hospital data. The insights could be delivered through a voice-activated product, possibly a reprogrammed version of the Amazon Echo or Google Home. Doctors and other staff could ask or provide information or data using voice recognition without holding a physical device like a tablet or smartphone.

Further, the system could easily encompass an entire health care facility by incorporating smaller "satellite" stations that offered access to the system at various locations. Is it possible to partner with a company like Google or Amazon to use their devices to deliver just-in-time information to any business? Absolutely!

You can see how this example functions on several levels. First, you're being anticipatory. Rearview Thinking might suggest just more of the same—if your equipment is overburdened, just buy more! Instead, you're looking at things in an entirely new light. Instead of "more," how can "different" better address the situation?

Moreover, the solutions that you're considering aren't locked into the here and now. Using the concept of a Soft Trend from chapter 2 here can help considerably. Growing patient loads and an increasing strain on hospital staff, particularly in settings such as the emergency room, represent a Soft Trend that can be influenced or changed. For example, you could partner with college students working toward a degree in software design or data science to help you develop a smartphone app that functions similarly to a Sirilike e-assistant. The app could be used either by a patient or by someone who is helping them get to the hospital by asking key questions and getting key information transmitted to the emergency room staff while they are en route. Hospital staff members would know when that patient should be treated—and whether someone else in the emergency room should be treated before the patient arrives at the hospital. Necessary medical forms could be automatically filled out—another time-saver.

The same e-assistant app could also notify a doctor that a post-operation patient's vitals are not where they should be—the doctor could automatically contact the patient and ask him or her to come in for a visit. Those and other solutions like them are not only proactive and cost-effective but reduce staff work levels at the same time.

Anticipation and innovation such as this can occur regardless of the setting or the person involved. As just one other example among many, a receptionist who notices that job interviews are taking longer than human resources would like might suggest an iPad presentation be given to every applicant who sits down in the waiting area. The five-minute video and interactive presentation could not only high-light primary facts about the company and its makeup but also offer an interactive FAQ feature that answers common questions. That not only trims time with HR personnel but makes the most use of what might otherwise be nothing more than nervous downtime for the applicant.

Building a Culture of Innovation

This discussion of the varied ways innovation can occur at any level highlights another misconception that can result from Rearview Mir-ror Thinking: that innovation in and of itself must always be on a grand scale.

As human beings, we readily embrace big innovations, the world-as-we-know-it game changers. After all, we camp out for days in advance to buy the latest smartphone! In part, this harkens back to the traditional view of who can innovate in the first place—only those in positions of authority who have the time and resources to embrace sig-nificant insights. Put another way, "those people" aren't going to waste their time coming up with an innovative solution just so job applicants don't take five more minutes in their interviews than they should!

As you can see, it's understandable why some people may believe this misconception. But the AO Model underscores the value of all forms of innovation, both those on a grand scale and those that are less sexy, for lack of a better term. By encouraging everyone within an organization to use anticipatory thinking and the tools we provide for accelerating problem-solving, transformation can not only occur at all levels within a company but at all levels of innovation as well—Every-day as well as Exponential.

Our prior example of using an iPad for interviewees is a great exam-ple of Everyday Innovation—not enormous in scope but very effective nonetheless. The example of a salesperson or hospital staff member suggesting a voice-activated Sirilike mobile app for recording patient data is another. The mobile device and the supercomputer that powers the e-assistant already exist—the innovative opportunity lies in how you can use those existing tools in an inventive way to solve an everyday, growing problem.

With those examples in mind, think about what you do every day. Is your job to keep your head down, do what you're supposed to do, and avoid any sort of innovative thought to solve both current and predictable problems? In the old days—even just five years ago—that might have worked, but not now, and not in the future. These days, we need to raise our heads up—and often—and look around with our antennas for predictable problems and new opportunities to improve what we do on a daily basis. There are going to be more problems coming our way at a faster rate in the years ahead. To keep from drowning in problems and turn change into an advantage, we need to identify predictable problems *before* we have to deal with them so that we can pre-solve them.

> **"By encouraging everyone within an organization to use anticipatory thinking and the tools we provide for accelerating problem-solving, transformation can not only occur at all levels within a company but at all levels of innovation as well—Everyday as well as Exponential."**

And we can. On one level, we all have a particular expertise or form of insight that we bring to our jobs. For instance, an accountant obviously knows how to accurately record and report what has happened during a specific period of time. A sales professional not only knows what they are selling but also how to overcome objections. A teacher, on the other hand, knows his or her subject; a really talented teacher knows how to convey that knowledge in an engaging way to students. We all have our strengths. Our subject area expertise positions and qualifies us to identify innovative solutions to the issues that we encounter all the time. In a sense, we're all at the front lines of what we do. This puts us in an optimal position to notice all sorts of opportunities for innovation.

There are also what I call crossover innovation opportunities. Just because each of us works in a particular field, discipline, or job doesn't preclude us from identifying predictable problems and innovation opportunities outside of our primary responsibilities and routines. We need to ignore those sorts of boundaries. Think back to my hypothetical example of a salesperson visiting a hospital. By being aware of Hard and Soft Trends, keeping your antenna up, and employing an Anticipatory Mindset, you can suggest innovations that are completely outside your formal training and expertise, such as ways to improve care and better handle growing patient loads.

> "When you look at something, ask yourself if you're thinking big enough. Is there a way you can take something to a much higher level at a faster pace? Those and other questions like them are the drivers behind both Exponential Innovation as well as Everyday Innovation—and are the result, as I mentioned earlier, of everyone keeping their antenna up, all the time."

Of course, there's also Exponential Innovation—innovation that's broader in scope as well as impact. These can be the real game changers—the iPhone, Uber, and other sorts of innovations that disrupt entire industries. The rub to this is not everyone in a company or organization is positioned to introduce Exponential Innovation—that often mandates a position of authority or influence.

Still, no matter if it's big or small innovation, by applying the AO Model, the thinking behind innovation remains the same. Consider this: When you look at something, ask yourself if you're thinking big enough. Is there a way you can take something to a much higher level at a faster pace? Those and other questions like them are the drivers behind both Exponential Innovation as well as Everyday Innovation—and are the result, as I mentioned earlier, of everyone keeping their antenna up, all the time.

The broader message is that not every type of innovation has to be an utter game changer. But by building a culture of anticipation, innovation can take place at every level of an organization's activities and functions—promoting a prevalent mindset that, over time, can prove every bit as valuable as any blockbuster-level innovation.

Eight Hard Trend Pathways to Innovation

To help you see invisible opportunities to innovate as well as understand the value and variety of innovation around you, it helps to understand the Eight Hard Trend Pathways to Innovation (covered in more substantive detail in our Anticipatory Organization Learning System). We touched on dematerialization and virtualization earlier in the chapter. Here are the remaining six pathways. These provide opportunities to drive both Everyday and Exponential Innovation:

- **Mobility.** Consider the rapidly growing global empowerment and economic development driven by the widespread adoption of smartphones and tablets. Add to that the software and mobile apps, which allow users to personalize their device by easily installing only the software they want, any time, any place, and without an IT department's help. And let's not forget the rapid growth of wearables and their expanding list of capabilities. There are countless processes that can be transformed and new services that can be provided by way of mobility.

- **Intelligence.** With the rapid growth of the Internet of Things (IoT), machines and sensors talking to machines, we can add networked intelligence to any product or service. In addition, artificial intelligence will get increasingly embedded into our products and services, providing expert guidance and an increasing ability to predict and prevent.

- **Networking.** Networking is increasing in scope and speed as well as in the new ways it can be used, such as networked sensors and machines, drones, and 3-D simulations. We're experiencing a greater level of connectivity all the time, and it's going to keep increasing. The future is wired, fiber, and wireless—and all are rapidly increasing in capacity.

- **Interactivity.** Thanks to the rapid advances of IPTV (Internet Protocol Television), the ability to add interactive features to products and services has never been easier. Think how interactivity can be used to transform everything from business processes to education to entertainment.

- **Globalization.** Technology enables globalization. In today's mobile, virtual, visual, and social world, it becomes easier every day to interact, sell, and buy from anyone, anywhere on the planet. In addition, there are different levels and forms of globalization, from manufacturing a product for the unique needs of a specific culture or geography to having foreign-born members on a board of directors.

- **Convergence.** You can converge features and functions to create added value. We've experienced this with devices such as our smartphones. Entire industries can also converge, as we have seen with the computer industry, the telecom industry, and the entertainment industry.

The beauty of using the Eight Hard Trend Pathways to identify and drive both Everyday and Exponential Innovation is that they effectively steer you away from a narrow view of how innovation can be applied. By that I mean unduly focusing on one pathway to the exclusion of others. For instance, you may initially look to mobility as an innovative solution for a particular issue, only to discover that virtu-alization can address the same problem but in a different and more efficient way. You may think a certain device may be suited to mobility, but its current form is too darn big. But dematerialization—making things smaller—is another pathway to innovation that can be used to overcome that problem.

Like so many things in the AO Model, there's synergy and an eco-system. Nothing exists in a vacuum. The Eight Hard Trend Pathways to Innovation are all the more powerful when working together. The beauty of these pathways is their inherent flexibility—you can use one by itself, in combination with others, or all of them together.

Additional Benefits of Accelerating Innovation

It's clear that a cultural environment that encourages innovation at all levels can produce amazing ideas and synergy. But there are other ben-efits as well. For one thing, an ongoing focus on actively looking for opportunities to innovate builds a sense of empowerment and engage-ment in everyone within a company or organization. Promoting an Anticipatory Mindset and encouraging an ever-present attention to innovation of all types fosters a greater sense of belonging and involve-ment for all.

Another buzzword is creativity. Creativity has traditionally been seen as a "soft skill"—some people are creative, and others aren't. Frankly, it's hard to simply instruct someone to "be more creative." What does that mean, and moreover, how do you do it? By contrast, The AO Model pro-vides tools that can help people be both creative and innovative. Apply-ing the Law of Opposites (which I will speak more about in the next chapter), identifying Soft Trends that can be influenced, and looking for a way to either redefine or reinvent a product or service are a few good examples. It's the function of having a process—which, as it happens, can lead to very creative innovation. In other words, innovation is a form of applied creativity—as much a process as it is a result.

Imagine you're the CEO of a large company, and you want to accelerate innovation. To that end, there may be a specialized group of people who are really good at identifying Hard and Soft Trends and, from there, identifying game-changing Exponential Innovation opportunities. Call them your Exponential Innovation team (a team, I might add, that makes a great addition to any company). But there's a bigger, broader form of innovation that can occur when there is also a focus on making Everyday Innovation part of corporate culture, with everyone practicing innovation in a continuous way by keeping their antennas up, identifying and solving problems before they occur, and spotting trends that offer actionable opportunity.

Is that the sort of company or organization you feel privileged to lead—one characterized by incremental innovation that leads to incremental results as well as Exponential Innovation that produces exponential results? You bet it is.

Chapter 5

Let Others Compete—
Move Beyond Competition

My brother was one of the first to notice it.

"You know, you just don't compete with anybody," he said to me one day, pretty much out of the blue. "You stack the deck. You get things so that, instead of copying someone else in any way, you purposely don't compete with them. You just move on to the predictable next level and do that instead."

I took that as a compliment, but I also gave it some thought. What did he mean? And, perhaps even more important, how could others benefit from it?

As I turned the topic over in my mind, I thought about how I compared myself with others. That's when the term benchmarking came to mind. Benchmarking means identifying the processes, systems, and technology, as well as the winning attributes of the services and products the leading companies in your industry are using to be the best, and then basically trying to copy what they are doing so that your company can achieve a leadership position like theirs.

But the flaw is, at best, you're only keeping up. As we've discussed, this is a fool's errand with little competitive advantage. In a time of continual transformation and technological change, merely trying to keep pace with the competition won't provide the sort of competitive advantage you used to enjoy. You may gain a bit of traction for a while, but sooner or later you're going to be stuck. In addition, if you are focusing on competing, you will be distracted from seeing new transformational opportunities, thus providing a window for startups and outsiders to focus on the future and use new processes and tools to move far beyond you.

The solution is to intentionally move beyond your competition. Focus on identifying the Hard Trends that are shaping the future and the Soft Trends you can positively influence. Redefine and reinvent your processes, services, and products before someone else does—let the others compete.

Beyond Competition

I used the principle of going beyond competition when I started an ultralight aviation company in 1980. I was attracted at first because of the way it reinvented aviation with modern materials—it began by attaching an engine to a hang glider frame—and I could see a growing new market. Most companies focused on two primary selling points: It was an inexpensive way to fly and did not require a pilot's license.

After building and flying what was considered to be one of the best powered hang gliders at the time, I soon realized that hang gliders were not designed to be powered. It was very easy to get into trouble fast, as evidenced by the rising number of fatalities that were occurring.

Instead of doing what everyone else was doing, I stopped and asked myself two important questions: What would the ideal ultralight look like? How would it function? Almost immediately I could see that it wouldn't fly like a hang glider using weight shifts for control—hang gliders were not designed for speed. An ideal ultralight would also need built-in pilot protection features to be safe.

After some research, I located and worked with a manufacturer who could build an ultralight with aircraft-quality parts. This ultralight had full three-axis control, which meant it flew like an airplane using a stick and rudder. It offered great pilot protection. From there, I did the opposite of what everyone else was doing. Instead of selling them to people who didn't have licenses—which I saw as high risk—I only sold to people with a pilot's license. Accordingly, I established a national network of dealers who were all flight instructors at smaller airports.

You can see how this all moved my ultralight business beyond the competition. Within the first year, I was a national leader in sales with a perfect safety record. Rather than compete with my peers by trying to sell a product that didn't require a license, I focused instead on active, fully licensed, fully qualified pilots who, given the routine of flying, may have become a bit bored. (Think of airline pilots flying at high altitudes with the autopilot handling the controls.) Our ultralights offered these pilots the opportunity to get back to enjoying flying low and slow again—and many bought our product as a result.

The more you focus on the competition, the more you will be tempted to adopt or adapt what they do, and that will only serve to make you look and act like them. For example, was Uber explicitly focused on competing with the cab industry when they launched their ride-sharing app? When Amazon launched the first virtual bookstore, were they focused on competing with other bookstores? No! They were aware of how others functioned—Uber knew how people hailed a taxi and had to fumble with their purse or wallet to pay for it, and Amazon knew how people shopped in bookstores. Instead of imitating, they innovated by intentionally focusing on what the competition was not doing. They went in the opposite direction and, in doing so, grew rapidly and moved beyond competition. They used new tools to redefine and reinvent rather than merely compete.

Redefining and Reinventing

Let me explain what I mean by redefining and reinventing. *Redefining* is seeing something in a different light or context. Given the Hard

Trends that we can be certain are shaping our future, how can we expand, reconfigure, or refocus something?

Reinventing, on the other hand, is broader in scope and impact. Once you reinvent something, you're harnessing the power of transformation. Whatever is reinvented is never going back to the way it was—particularly if you leverage some of the new, exponential tools available to you, such as the cloud, mobility, virtualization, artificial intelligence, and others. In other words, this isn't just a tweak or minor adjustment.

Given the rate of growth and change we're now experiencing, it's clear that we're living in an age of transformation. Competing under those sorts of accelerated conditions means merely keeping up at best—and falling far behind at worst. Neither is a means to survive, let alone thrive.

Think back to some of the examples we've cited in prior chapters. There are plenty of companies and organizations that merely tried to compete. Blockbuster tried to compete by expanding the number of stores as well as the number of movies it offered. What they didn't recognize is that the ultimate "location" is the phone in the palm of your hand. Dell tried to compete by doubling down on laptop sales. Their thinking—completely understandable—was that, since they had been successful competing in the past in laptop sales, simply upping their competitive game would keep them at the top of the heap. In a way, it's ironic. Dell recognized that consumers would welcome the opportunity to use a laptop instead of a desktop computer, only to miss the next critical phase—that those same consumers would happily abandon laptops in favor of smartphones and tablets.

Meanwhile, others were busy redefining and reinventing. Netflix looked at the Three Digital Accelerators and redefined how we watch movies by offering streaming services. Apple looked at Hard Trends and revolutionized the phone. They and others redefined, reinvented, and, in the end, disrupted entire industries.

Before we move into the mechanics of redefining and reinventing, two other points are important. First, redefining and reinventing are not just variations on a theme. It's not a matter of adding a feature, a twist, or a wrinkle to something. Rather, when something is redefined and reinvented, it's utterly changed. Since reinvention leverages the power of transformation, it's never going back to the way it was before. Since you can now stream thousands of movies, you're not going to drag yourself down to the video rental shop and dig through shelves. Since you can order an Uber and know exactly how much your fare will be, you're not going to automatically try to flag down a cab during rush hour, not knowing if the traffic will burn a hole in your wallet.

Additionally, don't treat the disruption that comes from redefining and reinvention as a one-shot deal. Think back to the early portion of the 21st century. Amazon had been around for more than 20 years, so brick-and-mortar retailers were accustomed to the disruption of someone being able to go online and shop. What else could happen? Mobile, that's what. Consumers were no longer chained to their desktop or laptop computers. They could shop online—and gain access to an exploding number and variety of items and the ability to quickly compare prices—from that minicomputer tucked into their pocket: their smartphone. In many cases, an order could arrive the very next day.

The message here is that disruption isn't a one-and-done proposition. If it happens once, chances are good it will happen again—often from a source that's utterly unexpected. With that sort of environment, merely trying to compete can doom you to consistently lag steps behind others—or worse.

In the past, reinventing was a powerful option. Today, it's an imperative. Given the breakneck acceleration in technological capability and capacity, the whole notion of stability has been stood on its head. Moreover, you cannot just reinvent now and then or when the mood strikes you. To survive and thrive, you have to constantly engage in the process of redefining and reinventing your products, your services, your businesses, and yourself.

How to Redefine and Reinvent

Although they may seem intimidating at first glance, redefining and reinventing are largely a matter of using tools and strategies we've already discussed. As is the case with other competencies, it's also a question of using more traditional skills in a different manner.

Let's take benchmarking, a concept we touched on earlier in this chapter. The problem with benchmarking is that focusing on identifying and implementing the best practices of industry leaders locks you into a pattern of playing catch-up with the best. By the time you implement the leader's best practices, they have already moved on. In other words, benchmarking has a present focus, not a future focus—and that's a bad thing in a time of technology-driven transformational change.

Redefining and reinventing take the concept of benchmarking and dramatically increase its competitive value. For instance, when I hear someone who is doing extremely well in something that I want to do well in, I might be tempted to say, "Wow, they are the industry leader, and they are getting fantastic results. I'll copy what they are doing, and, in time, I'll get to where they are." But this pattern of thought still puts me behind the curve. It's a lot like agility—it's good, but it doesn't help you jump ahead.

Instead, as an anticipatory thinker, consider the new transformational tools at hand. What are the Hard and Soft Trends I can leverage to redefine the current benchmark? How can I leap ahead not to merely change or tinker with how something is done but utterly reinvent it so that I can move beyond merely competing? Or, alternatively, what products, services, or processes need to be redefined or reinvented?

Here's an example of how redefining and reinventing a particular service might go. Let's say you're in charge of the benefits program for a large manufacturing company—several thousand employees. A major concern is health insurance costs—simply put, when people are sick, it's very expensive. The more they use their health insurance, the more it costs.

Your initial thought might be to trim benefits packages to hold down costs. But how about looking at it from a more anticipatory perspective? Many large companies have given their employees Fitbits as part of company-wide competitions to get in better shape. Employees are losing weight and getting their cholesterol under control to the point that they no longer need medication.

My sister is an executive for an international placement firm that is holding a competition to climb Mt. Everest. Of course, they're not actually climbing the mountain itself but measuring it by the number of steps they take, complete with a graphic of the mountain that allows you to see who's down in base camp and who's up above. It's amazing!

What's also amazing is that this exercise has resulted in fewer sick days and medication costs, which lowers their health care costs without requiring them to cut back on any employee benefits. They successfully utilized a transformative technology—in this case, wearables—to actually impact and change the future.

The Varied Views of Redefining and Reinventing

On the surface, the most obvious form of moving past the idea of competition and toward redefining and reinventing is directed externally—a focus on those other people, companies, and organizations with whom we used to compete.

But it's also advantageous to broaden that view a bit. For instance, one of the Eight Hard Trend Pathways to Innovation discussed in the Anticipatory Organization Learning System is convergence. As the name suggests, this represents certain things coming together— a powerful Hard Trend. On a small scale—physically, at least—you can recognize convergence in the number of different functions your smartphone can perform, from photography and high-quality video recording to GPS navigation and watching cable and television shows to using the Internet to access a world filled with information. Those and a large number of other functions used to be housed in separate devices—not any more!

Convergence is also occurring on a larger, industry-sized scale. Again, you can see this as various sorts of industries—such as telecommunications and consumer electronics—have come together into a single entity. A Hard Trend holds that this sort of large-scale convergence will continue in the future—both in industries that have already experienced significant convergence as well as those that have yet to do so.

That begs an anticipatory question: How will your industry be impacted by convergence? What industries will converge with your industry? What does the future look like? What Hard and Soft Trends can you identify to take advantage of any foreseeable convergence? What opportunities can you anticipate that will allow you to move forward and away from the idea of competition?

Moving back to an external standpoint, consider customers and clients as well. How will convergence impact the consumer? What sorts of industries will converge with your customers' industries? What sorts of services and products will they expect once convergence takes hold? How will prices be affected? Anticipating these questions can help you get a jump on others and move beyond competition yet again.

This also relates to a point I discussed earlier—the idea that, in the future, disruption may occur from surprising sources. By looking at industry-wide convergence, you're effectively anticipating where those new disruptors may come from, rather than just focusing on those companies of which you're aware. As I said, I'm less worried about the competitors who are currently in the picture than those invisible "competitors" who can come out of the blue with enormous disruptive force. Further, the visibility gained by anticipatory thinking also puts you in a position to *be* one of those disruptors.

Lastly, consider the issue of competition from an internal perspective by giving some thought as to how convergence and other Hard and Soft Trends may impact your particular company or organization. How will you be impacted on a purely internal basis? What products and services will be changed or rendered completely obsolete? What new opportunities can you identify from these fully predictable trends?

Look at this on an individual basis as well. How will you and your current job and responsibilities be impacted by Hard and Soft Trends? What can you be doing now in terms of training, education, and other steps to better position yourself to be more relevant and thrive in the years ahead?

All this moves you, your team, and your organization beyond the idea of competition. For instance, by giving careful thought as to how your job will be impacted by fully predictable Hard Trends, you can position yourself to move past competition with others. You're going beyond just trying to better some other salesperson's monthly sales tally or land a plum promotion instead of someone else. Instead, you're considering where things will be years in the future, where many opportunity-laden jobs that have yet to be developed will be available. You're not caught up in the battle of competition. You've eliminated the battle.

The Law of Opposites

Another way to move beyond the notion of competing is rather simple—if everyone is looking one way or at one particular thing, try looking in the opposite direction.

That's what I refer to as the Law of Opposites. In an era where innovation is an imperative, looking where no one else happens to be looking allows you to see what no one else can see and unlock enormous opportunities.

There are many examples of companies that leveraged the Law of Opposites to their advantage. Before Starbucks, coffee just happened to be an inexpensive "something else" on the table next to the bagel and cream cheese or roll and butter. Starbucks went in the opposite direction and began offering expensive, gourmet coffee drinks—some of which you could personalize yourself. They made coffee the focal point, rather than the afterthought.

As further proof of Starbucks' savvy use of the Law of Opposites, as of the writing of this book, the company had just opened its first store in Italy. Think about that. Conventional wisdom holds that quality coffee is best sold where there is none. Not by Starbucks' reckoning—they set up shop in a country where world-class espresso, cappuccino, and other coffee drinks are available on almost every street corner. Americans travel to Italy, and they love going to Starbucks—it's comforting and familiar. (The jury may still be out, but early reports suggest Italian Millennials are also attracted to the store—not just because it's new but also for the free Wi-Fi.)

Other examples of the Law of Opposites abound. It used to be that if you wanted to buy a new book, you had to go to a bookstore. Amazon changed that by allowing consumers to do the opposite and stay home, order their books online, and get instant delivery if it was an e-book and fast delivery if it was a traditional paper book. As Amazon expanded beyond books to sell just about everything online, they increasingly became a technology company using massive computing power and servers. Instead of keeping their entire computing and server infrastructure for themselves, they did the opposite and sold their excess capacity to customers as a virtual service.

The Law of Opposites lets you move beyond competition in other ways, too. Sometimes, it may spell the difference between mere irrelevancy and outright survival. For instance, if you're a small retailer, the idea of a Walmart moving into your community may be terrifying. Of course you can't compete with Walmart on price. Instead, do the opposite. Provide a better in-store service experience. Know your customers better than they can (an obvious advantage to being smaller). Provide more complete after-the-sale support. These and other strategies are not a form of competition—by offering services and products that Walmart does not, or does not do particularly well, you've skirted the entire issue of head-on competition.

This use of the Law of Opposites also ties in with another valuable means with which to redefine and reinvent—Problem Skipping. In a nutshell, this refers to the strategy of effectively bypassing what you may believe is your biggest problem or obstacle and identifying what, in fact, is the real problem. Once you have identified the real problem, it's much easier to identify a viable solution. In our Walmart example, the problem that was skipped was how to compete with a behemoth retailer whose most attractive selling point is low price— the solution was offering different, valuable services instead of going toe-to-toe with Walmart's biggest strengths. I'll be covering Problem Skipping in chapter 6.

Go Beyond Competition: Redefine Risk Management

Innovation is imperative in a constantly transforming environment. In the past, innovation was also inherently risky—a new product, service, direction, or other significant shift was weighed down with the uncertainty of the unknown.

> "When an organization embraces an Anticipatory Mindset, employees aren't nervous about posing potentially groundbreaking ideas out of fear of failure. They're effectively empowered with certainty."

With an Anticipatory Mindset, that level of risk simply need not be the case. Using Hard and Soft Trends, as well as other elements of the AO Model, we can better gauge and manage the risk level of innovation—and from there, make better and more informed choices. That's a complete redefinition of risk management.

Recall some of the issues we've discussed in this chapter:

- What Hard Trends will have a direct influence on your industry or company? What is the predictable impact they will have on your customers? What are the new opportunities you can use to elevate your competitive position with regard to your customers?

- What are the Soft Trends that you would like to see happen, such as increasing sales, and are they based on well-researched Hard Assumptions, or are they based on Soft Assumptions that just seem to make sense to you but, because they were not researched, carry much higher risk? What risks are involved with each and, by the same token, what are the opportunities to influence them?

Posing these and other questions allows us to correlate risk with opportunity and effectively better manage that opportunity. We can anticipate and pre-solve problems and overcome roadblocks in advance, thereby further reducing risk.

A common theme when I work with companies and organizations of all sorts is a preponderance of ideas. I hear time and again: "We're not lacking for ideas." The unspoken follow-up question is obvious: How do we know which ones are genuinely promising and those that might lead to disaster?

The answer is simple. By employing anticipatory thinking and examining ideas through the lens of Hard and Soft

> **"The benefits are pervasive. When an organization embraces an Anticipatory Mindset, employees aren't nervous about posing potentially groundbreaking ideas out of fear of failure. They're effectively empowered with certainty."**

Trends, you can separate unduly risky forms of innovation from those that are no less promising but a good deal less uncertain. For instance, is an innovative idea consistent with an established Hard Trend or does it run counter? That alone identifies relative risk.

The benefits are pervasive. When an organization embraces an Anticipatory Mindset, employees aren't nervous about posing potentially groundbreaking ideas out of fear of failure. They're effectively empowered with certainty. Further, by encouraging anticipatory thinking organization wide, leaders help others in the organization move beyond a "here today, gone tomorrow" assumption that many can have with regard to new strategies. Over the years, they've seen other leaders come and go, all with their particular agendas and ideas. They came and went and so, too, did their agendas and ideas.

As a leader, when introducing a new strategy or policy, be sure to tie it to a Hard Trend certainty so everyone recognizes that it is not based on a personal agenda. Rather, it is based on future facts—this trend will *not* pass. Embracing it is the only option. Using this approach empowers people with the confidence that certainty provides.

There's no way to eliminate risk completely. As I've said before, a risk-free, uncertainty-free world would be incredibly boring! But an Anticipatory Mindset and approach allows you to better manage risk, and from there, better identify and leverage all sorts of opportunities. This, along with a focus on redefining and reinventing processes, services, and products, can propel you and your organization beyond the competition.

Chapter 6

Applying the Skip It Principle

Here's a brief exercise I'd like you to try. Think of your biggest problem. It doesn't matter what it is—be it work related, at home, or having to do with family matters, whatever. Just think of the problem that you currently find most challenging or troubling.

Now, I'd like you to Skip It.

If you're like many people, that may seem a rather outrageous suggestion—or, at the very least, not a particularly constructive one. How, you may ask, does skipping a major problem help me? How does it get me closer to a solution?

To answer that in brief: You'll be pleasantly surprised at how much closer it can bring you to a solution—and how quickly.

Problem Skipping is one of the most effective and widely applicable elements of the overall AO model. Still, in working with various clients and in speaking to audiences, the reaction is often the same as yours might have been. Skip a problem? That would be great, but it wouldn't solve anything. Where's the good in that?

To address that question a bit more thoroughly than I just did, Problem Skipping is an exceedingly powerful strategy, not merely to accelerate growth and innovation but, ironically enough, as a means to address all sorts of problems that may have seemed utterly unsolvable.

What We Usually Do with Problems

Before I discuss the efficacy of Problem Skipping, it's helpful to address a preliminary issue. For many of us, Problem Skipping seems anything but constructive. Rather, it feels avoidant. By skipping a problem, you're not addressing it; you're just running away. Looked at in another way, "working the problem" instead of skipping it has been ingrained in us. *Everyone* does it.

Like so many other issues and strategies covered in this book, that's a mindset I'd like you to revisit. While many of us are geared toward taking problems head-on—often repeatedly—it's frequently an ineffective and unconstructive action. Think about a recent problem you encountered and how determined you were to work your way through it. The more energy you expended trying to push against it, the more this seemingly immovable object resisted. You wasted energy and—just as important—time. The problem kept you from moving forward. Still, you pressed on, immersed in your conviction that problems are meant to be taken head-on—over and over, if necessary.

That's because you weren't aware that you can skip them—and why it's so effective to do so. Moreover, there is a proven way to do this, no matter how overwhelming the problem might seem to be.

Skip It to Find the Real Problem

There are two types of Problem Skipping, both of which can be critical to accelerating innovation and success. The first is skipping what you thought was the problem so that you can identify the *real* problem and ultimately find the solution you seek.

The basic point here is that, in confronting a perceived problem, many of us effectively misidentify the problem that we think we need to solve. This is particularly true with a problem that, at first glance, seems utterly enormous and intimidating—the kind of problem that doesn't seem to have a solution at all.

But the reason the problem or challenge is so big and seemingly unsolvable is that it's not defined correctly. Moreover, if it were the correct problem, wouldn't it stand to reason that you would have solved it by now, given all the time and effort you have put into it?

Here's an anecdote that illustrates what I'm getting at. In the furniture industry, most major sales are typically held in November or December. As a result, manufacturers look to stockpile inventory for these major year-end events. The problem is often storage—as inventory accumulates, many furniture companies assume they need to build bigger warehouses to store it all.

The answer: Skip It. One furniture manufacturer I know offered incentives to encourage stores to stock the additional inventory on site. It worked great! Not only did the company avoid having to build additional storage space, with so much inventory readily available, retail stores sold more throughout the year in addition to their year-end sales.

That's a classic example of skipping the problem you think is the one that matters and redirecting your efforts toward uncovering the real issue. The furniture manufacturer's real problem was that they had identified the wrong problem from the very start—the need to build more warehouses.

When we see a problem, we have a tendency to take it at face value. Put another way, "That's the problem I see first, so it must be the one I need to address."

But to effectively identify and address the real problem, it's imperative to do some Problem Skipping. Peel back the onion a bit, then a bit more. Ask a few why questions. In the furniture manufacturer's case, it would start with the question: Why do we need to build more warehouses? The answer is: Retailers sell most of their stock without ordering ahead of time. Next question would be: Why don't they want to carry more inventory? And so on, until the real problem is identified—and from there, a ready solution.

The furniture manufacturer shouldn't feel particularly lonely in his surprise about the powers of Problem Skipping. I often talk with CEOs from every industry who insist they've identified a major problem only to discover later that they were wasting time and money chasing after the wrong thing. It's like taking your damaged car into the repair shop and going into exhaustive detail about whether it was a Chevy or a Ford that cut you off on the highway. Either may be true, but who cares? That's Rearview Mirror Thinking. The real problem is examining the resulting damage and mapping out a plan to repair it.

Here's another quick example—one involving another important principle I'll discuss in greater detail later in the book. I was chatting with the fellow who is in charge of a major lawn and tractor manufacturer dealer network. He explained that he wanted to shift dealers away from being "order takers"—customers come in looking for a tractor or a combine, and the dealers sell it to them. Instead, they wanted to encourage dealers to sell "solutions"—data analytics and other technology that, for instance, monitored production data so that farmers would know precisely which sections of their property yielded the best harvests.

The problem was that, no matter how corporate tried to urge dealers to sell solutions, they inevitably reverted back to being order takers. I asked him about their compensation structure. That's when the light came on. He explained that dealers received substantial commissions for selling combines and other equipment and less money for sales of more comprehensive, technology-tied solutions since their economic value increases with use.

That pinpointed the real problem—not the total system structure as such, but compensation. Reward the dealers for the total solution, not just the tangible unit itself, and the issue of getting them to sell total solutions would take care of itself.

I find this element of the AO Model particularly rewarding. I've always enjoyed sharing the principle of Problem Skipping and the reaction many people have when they understand how valuable it can be. In a way, it's not only enormously practical but also almost liberating. It frees you to consider solutions to underlying problems, rather than merely running head-on into one solution after another that doesn't work. It's like having the shackles removed. You're free to move forward.

Skip It Completely

As I said, there are two versions of Problem Skipping. The first is skipping the perceived problem so that you can find the real one. The second type is skipping the problem completely.

Here's an illustrative example. Since much of the population lives in isolated villages, African countries such as Rwanda have struggled to supply their citizens with medical supplies and other essential goods and services. But building a network of reliable roads would not only be time-consuming but prohibitively expensive.

The Skip It solution: The government looks to use drones to connect with far-flung villages, skipping the need to build roads. Additionally, African nations are looking to inexpensive smartphones to skip the need for a network of brick-and-mortar banks and using learning apps to address a patchy education system.

That's the basic concept of Problem Skipping: choosing to simply jump over a particular problem, issue, or barrier. Again, it's a question of unraveling accepted mindsets. We often assume that every single step is necessary to achieve a particular goal or success. Therefore, the accepted thinking is to take every one of those steps in order—first A, then B, C, and so on.

But that's not always necessary—in fact, it's frequently not. We think we need to do something, but we really don't. For instance, let's say I'm starting a company, and I need to get funding. Conventional thinking would suggest going to a bank for a loan or talking to venture capitalists or taking some other step to get funding prior to actually offering a service or product. Instead, how about skipping that and obtaining funding from your first major client—having them pay for first versions at a discount. Alternatively, how about using crowdsourcing?

Some additional examples follow:

- A small-business owner is deluged with new product orders but can't get the necessary funding to boost production. He skips the problem by preselling the products with a special benefit such as personalization—that fills the funding requirements needed to meet demand.

- Carbon dioxide is a primary culprit in global warming, but efforts to reduce it to date have been cumbersome and expensive. In an ideal example of Problem Skipping, a startup has developed a methodology to recycle carbon dioxide into a chemical that can be used to produce consumer products. They skipped advertising by developing a newsworthy story, giving them free national advertising.

Like the first version of Problem Skipping—one involving the misidentification of the actual problem at hand—Problem Skipping is a liberating experience. Rather than struggling unsuccessfully to pin down a problem that resists being pinned down, simply bypass it. In the process, you may discover that the problem really never warranted any attention or energy to begin with.

Another way to Problem Skip is to effectively break down an existing problem into a number of smaller components. Here's an example. Let's say you have a proposal in hand for a substantial, expensive project for your organization. In most cases, that means it has to wind its way through the system, being approved by various layers and individuals. It's got to go through legal. It's got to go through finance—probably multiple times.

Rather than just sending the entire proposal through the system as a big, expensive whole, how about breaking it into smaller, less expansive elements that can be quickly approved? The legal element of the proposal may not be needed at all by many divisions, reducing the time and money required to circulate the proposal. By subdividing the larger proposal into less involved and less expensive components, those varied people and groups involved in the overall process can lend their approval much quicker. In the end, once the varied components have been reassembled, you still have your original proposal—only with the stamp of approval without a lengthy wait.

Accelerate Success

The examples I shared above illustrate a central benefit of Problem Skipping in all forms. Simply put, by skipping the perceived problem or skipping it altogether, you're accelerating your success. Like the proposal that's broken down into smaller components only to reemerge at the other end, you emerge from problem skipping with the objective or goals you always had in mind—only a great deal faster than you would have had you stopped to wrestle with problems that, in the end, may have precluded success altogether.

Again, this isn't about avoiding or disregarding significant problems or barriers. Rather, it's just a different and more effective way of approaching them, a sort of conceptual jujitsu that sheds fresh light, often showing that our "required" actions can actually be skipped altogether to get to the same or better results with much greater speed. It's like wondering why you aren't going anywhere and then realizing you have your left foot on the brake and your right foot on the accelerator.

Here are some additional questions to help you grasp and appreciate the remarkable results available by way of Problem Skipping:

- Are you solving the right problem? Is the problem correctly defined?

- Does your problem statement actually contain multiple problems? Whenever you have more than one problem in a problem statement, the solution will be too complex and seldom works.

- Are there parts of a plan you could skip? Often, we do things that we think we need to do because that's how we've always done them. Are there ways to skip many of the things you think you need to do to move forward faster?

- Is there a way to use new technology to either rapidly solve or skip a problem area?

- Are you dealing with problems that you could easily skip just because that's the way everybody else does it? Are you just mimicking the behavior of others?

To reiterate, the idea of Problem Skipping may strike some as uncomfortable at first. In that sense, it's in line with many other concepts in this book. You're being encouraged to go against normal ways of thinking. But taken in concert with other AO principles—as well as the practical exercises outlined in the online AO program—you'll find yourself viewing your future and the ways in which you solve problems and accelerate your success, much differently.

To wrap up, here's a famous phrase that everybody has heard: You don't want to work harder; you want to work smarter. That's an excellent summation of Problem Skipping. Rather than assuming that hard, conventional, regimented work is the only means to accelerate success, sometimes it's a matter of taking more thoughtful, smarter approaches. It's not avoiding a problem; rather, it's a way to make faster progress toward a solution.

Chapter 7

Identifying and Developing Game-Changing Opportunities

At this point, you've learned how to anticipate disruption, problems, and opportunities by separating Hard Trends from Soft Trends and how to use the concepts of Redefining and Reinventing to turn change into an advantage, as well as other important lessons. These and other topics, such as the Three Digital Accelerators, represent the core of the AO Model—the ability to anticipate future events with remarkable accuracy and, from there, to plan for both Everyday Innovation as well as Exponential Innovation. Now it's time for us to start mining the opportunities and uncover the jewels that will shape your future.

The overriding importance of understanding why and how the varied elements of the AO Model work in such close coordination together is simple: Remove any one or several from the model, and you limit your ability to create extraordinary results.

On the other hand, bringing these strategies together and using them in a thoughtful, coordinated manner allows you to identify the best opportunities, accelerate innovation, and elevate results. You become what I refer to as an Opportunity Manager.

How is that defined? An Opportunity Manager goes beyond reacting quickly to change by actively looking for Hard Trends that are shaping the future. From there, she identifies related opportunities, refines them, and then acts on the opportunity that offers the biggest advantage. In that regard, it's not a matter of changing job definitions so much as it is looking for new opportunity as you elevate the relevancy of your current role.

As you'll see, this is very different from being a crisis manager. Don't misunderstand—you're still going to be managing crises. But at the same time, you'll be building your skills as an Opportunity Manager—someone who has their antenna up, looks for opportunities in new ways, and is adept at identifying and refining opportunities and pinpointing risk and reward. You'll also be able to manage crises faster by anticipating problems and pre-solving them in many cases.

Baby Boomers Retiring—So What?

An effective way to lay out the synergy between various elements of the AO Model is to return to a Hard Trend we've discussed before—the number of Baby Boomers in the United States. It goes without saying that the 78 million Boomers in this country will get older. That is a Hard Trend, pure and simple.

But, trends need to have value; they need to be connected to an opportunity. So, if you see the Hard Trend that Baby Boomers will be retiring in large numbers, so what? This is news? The point here is that a Hard or Soft Trend has far less strategic value if it isn't tied to an actionable opportunity. In the example of Baby Boomers, they're not merely getting older, but they're also retiring at a remarkably fast rate. And as I mentioned in a previous chapter, retiring with them is the knowledge, experience, and wisdom they've accumulated during decades of work. That loss of valuable experience is a Soft Trend that is likely, but it is also something that is open to influence.

That access to influence represents opportunity—something that the

Hard Trend of Baby Boomers retiring cannot offer in and of itself. It also emphasizes the importance of examining Hard and Soft Trends in the framework of consistently keeping an eye peeled for opportunities we can anticipate. In the case of Baby Boomers retiring, once they're out the door, the opportunity related to their knowledge and experience can largely go out the door with them. But, thinking in an anticipatory manner, what about establishing a comprehensive mentoring program before they retire through which they can pass along their skills and insights to their younger colleagues? What if their insights and success principles were shared on a dynamic, internal knowledge base? That's not merely being anticipatory—it's also being aware of the importance of connecting trends of all sorts to relevant and significant opportunity.

Further, by applying the Redefining and Reinventing Principle to a mentoring program, you can elevate its impact. For example, when most of us think of a mentor, we think of an older, experienced person, working one-on-one very closely with someone else, usually someone younger and less experienced. That's a great model, one whose value and importance have been established and reinforced over the course of centuries.

But even a "conventional" one-on-one mentoring relationship can be broadened. I know of a real-life example. I'm acquainted with a young PhD at a biotech company based in San Diego. I once asked him if the firm had any sort of mentoring program. They did, he said. In fact, he had seven mentors!

Intrigued, I asked him if all seven were in the specific division of the company in which he worked. No, he replied. In fact, some of them weren't even in the company at all. Some were customers, and others were vendors.

Now he really had my attention! I asked how often he was in touch with them. Weekly, he answered—with every single one of them. Granted, some were very brief conversations or just an email, but contact nonetheless.

To my mind, this was truly game-changing as well as representative of the kind of redefining and reinvention I discussed earlier. Not only was my young friend being anticipatory by tapping into the minds of older, more experienced colleagues and associates, he was doing so across professional disciplines, backgrounds, and other parameters.

By taking that single one-on-one model and multiplying it by a greater number of people on both sides of the formula—the mentors as well as the mentees—the potential and benefits are greatly amplified. The expanded synergy, sharing of knowledge and experience, and back-and-forth interplay that characterize a one mentor/one mentee model would benefit participants as well as an entire organization through the retention of knowledge and wisdom. It could result in the creation of a wisdom and knowledge base—a central repository.

Further, that wisdom database could be constantly dynamic. Actionable knowledge could be added, accessed, corrected, and discussed by everyone within an organization. Knowledge needs to be in motion to be of value—a static database offers little by comparison. By contrast, dynamic knowledge is not only in constant use, but it's also constantly being improved and broadened, furthering both the scope of its use as well as its value.

Again, this comes back to the idea of the inherent synergy of opportunity. Hard Trends and Soft Trends are everywhere for those who have learned to see them. But it's necessary to connect them with urgency and action. That's being an Opportunity Manager.

Managing and Prioritizing Opportunity

The term Opportunity Manager means just what it seems—you're not merely identifying opportunities of all sorts, you're managing them and leveraging them to your advantage. In other words, you're controlling the opportunity and not the other way around.

As we covered, part of being an effective Opportunity Manager is recognizing the interplay of varied elements of the AO Model. As is the case with so much we've discussed, nothing operates—let alone flourishes—in a vacuum. That's particularly true with your approach to effective Opportunity Management.

But all opportunity is not created equal. Part of being a truly effective Opportunity Manager is identifying and selecting those opportunities with the largest potential payoff and the least amount of risk and financial commitment. That means it's helpful to rank and prioritize various opportunities.

On one level, prioritizing translates to the level of importance and time frame. For instance, a particular opportunity might be vital to the growth of your business or organization. That, in turn, would suggest immediate action. By contrast, another opportunity might be potentially very beneficial, but the timeline for action isn't quite so constrained. That would indicate a secondary ranking, for lack of a better way to phrase it—an item or action that can be addressed effectively within the next two or three months or thereabouts. The third and final type of opportunity could be very valuable, but the time frame for action allows for a good deal of leeway—say, up to 12 months or more.

Another way to approach opportunity is the anticipated benefit. For instance, there are opportunities that might have a short time frame for execution and offer a significant payoff. By contrast, there are other options that involve a good deal more effort over a longer period of time to create a truly disruptive product or service that would mandate a good deal of planning and testing to ensure success. Here, the effort and time necessary for successful execution might be long and involved. The payoff may be significant, but would take a longer time to accomplish.

This is not to say that one sort of opportunity is necessarily better than another—far from it. Rather, opportunities come in varied forms and mandate different levels of effort, commitment, and time. Knowing that these varied choices exist and managing them in concert with one another is just another strategy employed by a successful Opportunity Manager.

This sort of opportunity management also impacts planning. Not very long ago, companies and organizations could develop and implement plans that might be applicable for a decade or more. Given the rate of change we're experiencing now, opportunities have a much narrower window—just look at how quickly flip phones have been overtaken by smartphones! That means many plans are bound to end up on the scrap heap of obsolescence—being of little use in a very short amount of time.

An Opportunity Manager is aware of this greatly condensed life-cycle and is constantly building and reviewing plans over a shorter time frame. As we've discussed, some may, in fact, take a long while to evolve and produce results. Others occur much more quickly. An Opportunity Manager is aware of this mix of time frames and opportunities and diversifies his planning accordingly.

Looking for Disruption with Intent

Predictable disruptions can offer the most valuable form of opportunity—the types of opportunities that upend an entire industry, bona fide game changers. When watching for disruptive opportunities, never lose sight of powerful Hard Trends that can produce disruptive opportunities with enormous potential.

We've already covered a number of these—demographics, government regulations, and the constant influx of new technology, among others. It's valuable to watch these and other Hard Trends with what I refer to as "disruptive intent." Is there a governmental issue, such as the necessity to develop and implement regulations governing drones or autonomous vehicles, that offers a powerful opportunity for disruption—to completely stand the status quo on its ear?

Demographics are another fertile area for disruption. For instance, demographics show that women are woefully underrepresented in a variety of technological fields. Given that, what might the opportunities for disruption be if a particular company became widely known as a desirable location for women to advance in a previously male-dominated field? That could mean an ability to recruit and retain a remarkable talent pool—and from that, drive both Everyday and Exponential Innovation.

Opportunity can also come in the form of pervasive problems. Are there any Hard Trends that come in the form of a particular challenge? For instance, the necessity of shifting to cloud computing and virtual servers is an ideal example of a widespread problem for many organizations. How can this problem be addressed effectively and, in turn, generate new disruptive opportunity?

Keep an eye on your customers as well. As the end user of your products and services, they can help identify disruptive opportunity. For instance, based on what they are doing now, as well as what they may be doing in the future, what sorts of problems and issues will they face? Are there any Hard Trends that will disrupt their current business model? Solicit their feedback. From there, how can you develop solutions before those sorts of problems become prevalent?

Additionally, don't overlook the Eight Hard Trend Pathways to Innovation, (listed on page 60) not merely as a means of solving customers' problems but as a way of identifying and leveraging disruptive opportunity. To use a previous example, is there a technology or tool that would have greater value if it were smaller? For instance, engineers at the University of Cambridge have developed an engine that is so small it can be placed inside a living cell! Similarly, so-called "Cube-Sats"—smaller versions of satellites—are being employed in space to offer the commercial and scientific services of much larger satellites but at a much lower cost.

These and other strategies are varied types of "lenses"—ways in which opportunity for disruption can be seen, identified, and sufficiently magnified to suggest a means of addressing them. They also help delineate various levels of opportunity. Some may be little more than a shift in the status quo, while others are outright game changers.

Soft Trends—Some Desirable, Some Not

As you may recall from chapter 2, all Soft Trends are based on assumptions—Hard Assumptions, which derive from data that can be supported, and Soft Assumptions, which boil down to more of a gut feeling about something. A Soft Trend that derives from a Hard Assumption carries less risk, while Soft Assumptions have a greater amount of uncertainty.

In terms of using Soft Trends of all sorts to become an Opportunity Manager, there are two other sorts of Soft Trend classifications to bear in mind: those Soft Trends that we want to see happen (longer lifespans, better overall health, increasing sales) and those that we want to change (increasing obesity or declining sales). Both can offer enormous opportunity, although our approach to them can be decidedly different.

On the one hand, there are the Soft Trends we like, such as people living longer. Bear in mind, of course, that there's an upside as well as a downside to every trend—that means it's valuable to view every Soft Trend in terms of both positive and negative consequences to identify opportunities that derive from both. Given the Soft Trend of people living longer, what opportunities are available to help ensure not just a longer life but a healthier and more rewarding life? What can we offer to help make those longer lives better, more fulfilling, and characterized more by good health rather than a rash of medical issues? In effect, an Opportunity Manager actively influences and works to boost a positive Soft Trend rather than doing anything to counter it.

On the other hand, there are Soft Trends that are a good deal less appealing. These can include such trends as increases in cybercrime, more frequent and damaging security breaches, increases in medical costs, and other similar issues and events. In this case, the opportunity afforded by the Soft Trend is more solution oriented. Unlike Soft Trends we like, we don't want to accentuate or accelerate a negative trend; we're looking for opportunities to reverse it, such as using behavioral analytics to reduce cybercrime or offering incentives for electric vehicles to slow down global warming. As an example of the former, many companies have challenged hackers to uncover security breaches and reward those who pinpoint the most vulnerable spots in their security networks.

The message here is that managing opportunities isn't confined to either the positive or, for that matter, to problems that mandate solutions. An Opportunity Manager looks for both, as those Soft Trends that we like and dislike can both offer significant opportunity.

Moreover, it's important to approach positive and negative Soft Trends with the same sort of analytic framework. First, where's the low-hanging fruit—those opportunities that offer a significant payback over a short period of time? By the same token, what Soft Trends— be they positive or negative—warrant a longer-term commitment or, alternatively, can be addressed with a lesser sense of immediacy? Additionally, is the opportunity internal or one more focused externally on clients or something else outside of your organization, such as shifting demographics of your employees or customers?

It's also valuable to strike a balance between short-term opportunities and other Soft Trends that will take longer to influence and come to fruition. Starting people on projects that are low-hanging fruit allows for a quick payoff—and, at the same time, encourages commit-ment to staying the course with those opportunities that have a longer time frame.

Lastly, be sure to analyze the assumption underlying all Soft Trends. A Hard Assumption affords greater confidence and less risk; a Soft Assumption means less confidence and a greater level of risk. Upon further examination, is what appeared to be a Hard Assumption actu-ally a Soft Assumption, or vice versa? Knowing and identifying one from the other can mean the difference between an opportunity seized or time and energy ill-used or misdirected entirely.

Your Past Success Didn't Depend on Being Anticipatory—Your Future Success Does

The heading of the final section of this chapter summarizes the essen-tial value of being an Opportunity Manager. Simply put, in the past, you could succeed without being anticipatory. The future offers no such option—being anticipatory is essential. The exponential speed and arc of change that we will continue to experience will ensure the necessity of that competency.

That's why the crux of this chapter has been the importance of looking for and acting on the sorts of opportunities that technological transformation afford us all. In the past, being a "reactor" was suf-ficient—you encountered certain issues, developments, and other events, and you reacted to them as best you could. Learning to be agile by reacting faster is better, but no longer good enough. It's far better (and necessary) to be an Opportunity Manager—someone who not only identifies opportunity but leverages it, directs it, and moves it in whatever direction offers the greatest rewards. The Opportunity Manager can direct change from the inside out, which we can control, rather than change from the outside in. This forces us to react.

As I've mentioned previously, becoming an Opportunity Manager doesn't spell the end of all uncertainty. It doesn't mean there won't be any future crises that need to be handled. What it does allow you is sufficient predictability to make a real difference in your future and the future of those around you. Developing the skills to become an Opportunity Manager also allows you to elevate your view of the future. That directly impacts how you act in the present, which in turn will directly shape your future. That's the topic we'll tackle in the next chapter.

SHAPE THE FUTURE—
TRANSFORM CULTURE

Chapter 8

Elevate Your View of the Future

I'm constantly surprised that we don't spend more time thinking about and planning for the future. After all, as I mentioned previously, that's where we're going to be spending the rest of our lives.

How you view the future impacts much more of the present than many of us realize. In developing and leveraging an Anticipatory Mindset, it's important to understand that the future doesn't function in a vacuum. Rather, it's something of a two-way street. While how you act in the present determines your future, so, too, does your view of the future impact how you think and act in the present.

This all has to do with the principle I call Futureview®. We all have a Futureview, although we view the future in different ways. What you choose to see and do can have a powerful impact on you and your organization, both now and in the future.

Futureview Defined

I developed the principle of Futureview back in the early 1980s. In brief, how you view the future shapes how you act in the present; further, how you act in the present shapes your future. In other words, your Futureview will determine the future you. This naturally raises the question: Is your Futureview based on a world that is ceasing to exist? Are you looking at the future with a windshield view that faces forward or a Rearview Mirror Mindset?

In one respect, Futureview is a very personal, singularly focused principle. For instance, right now there are people who are buying Facebook stock. At the same time, there are also people who are selling Facebook stock. The difference between these two sets of people is their Futureview of Facebook. Although decisions to buy or sell stock can have all sorts of reasons behind them, at their core is the investor's view of the company's prospects. Buyers generally have an optimistic view of a company's future, while sellers, for the most part, have a more negative outlook.

Futureview has a powerful impact on every type and size of organization. If you run a business, ask yourself: Are there customers or clients who are thinking about taking their business to another company? Why? Their Futureview of doing business with you is negative. On the other hand, there are customers who are planning on remaining, as their view of doing business with you now and in the future is positive. Again, the difference between the two groups is their Futureview of conducting business with you.

Futureview is a powerful force inside your organization as well. For instance, right now, you likely have talented employees who are surreptitiously looking for new jobs on LinkedIn and through any number of other employment options and services. At the same time—just a few cubicles away or on a different floor—there are also top-notch employees who can't wait to come to work and are so enthusiastic about your company's prospects that they wouldn't dream of working anywhere else.

This isn't necessarily about money (although it certainly can be). It can also be focused on the varied Futureviews that employees hold of your company. Some, such as the ones answering want ads and slyly circulating their resumes, probably don't have much optimism about the future of your company or their place in it. On the other hand, the "lifers" probably hold a glowing view of the future of the company and how they stand to benefit if they stay where they are.

These and other examples illustrate the role Futureview can play in all areas of our lives. If the prevailing Futureview is a positive one—such as those of the employees who wouldn't even consider changing jobs—your thoughts and actions, as well as theirs, in the present will reflect greater motivation and engagement. Maybe those positive-minded workers will perform their jobs at a particularly high level. As a result, not only will your company's future benefit, so, too, will those employees as they enjoy promotions and raises in salary.

The same holds true for a negative Futureview. If employees don't have a positive Futureview of your company, their actions in the present will be less engaged and motivated. Since they can't see themselves working for your company for too much longer, they may not bring a great deal of energy and commitment to their current job responsibilities. Their future may be better served by finding a job somewhere else.

Boiled down, your Futureview will determine the future you. At the same time, it also impacts the kind of person you are today.

Futureview: Causes and Effects

As you can tell, having a Futureview that's less than optimistic can be damaging on several levels. That begs the obvious question: Since it can be so problematic, how does someone come to acquire a negative Futureview or one that's simply outdated or obsolete?

Much of the cause boils down to a principle I've discussed previously—Rearview Mirror Thinking. To refresh your memory, Rearview Mirror Thinking looks to the future with yesterday's thinking. Your past experience acts as an anchor, holding back progress. As an example, if you're a retailer and your Futureview of brick-and-mortar operations is negative due to the increase of online sales—in effect, that the good old days of retail are behind you—your view of the future reflects that. Without a perspective based on the future, all you can do is have a negative Futureview. As a result, your thoughts and actions in the present will also reflect that and actively shape the future for you.

I don't mean to single out retailers. Rearview Mirror Thinking can negatively impact all sorts of companies, organizations, and even industries, from health care to transportation to education. That's because Rearview Mirror Thinking can, in effect, create an inaccurate Futureview. That's tragic, given the mountain of opportunity to create positive change that's there for us to see and act on. Rearview Mirror Thinking can mean that our future will most likely be far less than it could have been if it had been more aligned with future facts— the Hard Trends that are shaping the future and revealing amazing opportunities and a mountain of innovative promise. Once you see the opportunities using an Anticipatory Mindset, your actions will change and so will your future.

Futureview can become particularly important when examined on an organization-wide scale. No matter what the size of a company or organization, a shared Futureview is a unifier. It pulls people together by providing both clarity and focus around future goals and possibilities.

Futureview is also broader in scope than either a mission or vision statement. A mission statement outlines an organization's purpose, while a vision statement identifies an organization's road map and objectives, and is used to direct internal decision-making.

Mission and vision statements are valuable but have significant drawbacks. For one thing, chances are good most people don't know what their organization's mission or vision statement is—or they simply take them for the same thing. That means the statements don't help shape their thinking and behavior. Further, statements usually remain unchanged for long periods of time. Given the transformational changes we are experiencing now and in the future, that means they often represent Rearview Mirror Thinking. They really don't reflect the new future.

By contrast, a shared Futureview elevates attitude. Each of us possesses it, whether we know it or not! It has a direct impact on our daily actions. Rather than working at odds with others within the group, a common Futureview builds a sense of energy, empowerment, and a pervasive attention to the enormous opportunities in the days ahead. It provides the shared confidence that fosters bold moves.

On the other hand, having widely different views of the future can be problematic, if not downright destructive. If the people within a company or organization have a scattered view of the future, they're out of alignment. Since they, as individuals, all see different futures for your organization, the focus and clarity necessary to pull people together simply won't exist.

Here's an example. When I was working with a major German car manufacturer, I encouraged the CEO to solicit his employees' view of the future. They all did so in writing, and what he saw shocked him. Employees' Futureviews of the company were all over the board—there was almost no consistency or unity at all. For a car company geared toward moving into the future, their scattered Futureview was like trying to accelerate with the parking brake on and no clear destination.

Taking this point a step further, they naturally had a strategic plan—but, as we just noted, it didn't result in a shared Futureview. Additionally, after I reviewed their strategic plan, it was clear that it didn't take into account the transformational changes that were completely disrupting the automotive manufacturing industry. Put another way, even if they did have a shared Futureview, it was based on a future that was ceasing to exist, one that was no longer heading in the direction of the actual future. The future always changes, and if you keep moving toward the old future, you'll certainly get there—but without customers.

Products, services, and processes can all be copied or mimicked from one organization to another. The competitive advantage Futureview introduces is a culture with a shared mindset, which is far more difficult to replicate. Your organization's culture simply can't be copied—it's singularly unique. That's why there's a powerful advantage when you align an anticipatory culture with a shared Futureview. On the other hand, a scattered or past-oriented Futureview can literally defocus and even shred an organization's culture.

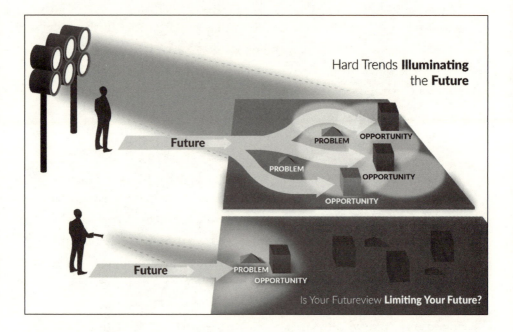

A shared, positive Futureview, based on the certainty that Hard Trends shaping the future provide, is pervasive. For instance, when looking at the future, we all have a tendency to focus on the technological advances we see every day. That's understandable, but because what we are doing today was impossible just a few years ago, and in two years we'll be doing something that was impossible today, it's imperative to have an Anticipatory Mindset. The real issue of value is how we put those tools—both today's and tomorrow's—to creative use. That's where mindset comes into play in another powerful way. All the wonderful tools in the world are of little value to an organization if the people within that group don't share a common Futureview and an Anticipatory Mindset with which they use those tools. This offers a competitive advantage that promotes Exponential Innovation while others are forced to react and imitate.

Further, a shared Futureview should not be limited to the people within your organization. To accelerate success, customers, vendors, strategic partners, allies, and sales agents should all have a shared Futureview. If they share the same positive Futureview as you, one that is focused on collaborating to cocreating a positive future, their actions will be aligned with yours, and the results will be amplified. That produces a powerful, focused synergy. As a result, you will all get to the future faster. You will lead, not follow.

Developing an Organization-Wide Futureview

Since an organization characterized by a shared Futureview can promote powerful innovation and energy on all levels, that raises the next question: How can you build and nurture an organization where everyone has a positive, shared Futureview?

It can be helpful to examine your company or organization with an eye toward your relationship with Hard Trends. First, identify those Hard Trends that are shaping the future of your organization, your industry, and your products and services. From there, consider: Is your Futureview aligned with those powerful forces? For instance, if you're involved with customer service, can your customers download an intelligent mobile app they can use to obtain answers and guidance whenever they want? Are you using AI and digital e-assistants that are branded for your company and customized for your customers to provide focused help around the clock?

Another way to approach your organization's shared Futureview is by examining everyday activity. A positive, shared Futureview that's based on the trends shaping the future is creating positive, directed change from the inside out. By contrast, an organization whose Futureview is not aligned is more reactionary by default—constantly reacting and responding to events and conditions coming from the outside in.

An organization with a shared, constructive Futureview is also one in which communication is stressed. If the leadership of a company or organization has an optimistic Futureview, not only do they make certain that it's a working part of their organization's function and culture, but they also communicate it to everyone else in the group. In effect they say: This is where we're going, this is why we're so excited, and this is why we want to make certain you share this view as well.

This is very constructive in more than one way. By communicating the importance and overriding message of Futureview, you're also building an inclusive organization. In effect, you're telling others that you value them and want them to be aware of and actively participate in your effort and enthusiasm regarding your shared Futureview. That mindset also encourages talented people to stay and grow with your organization rather than looking elsewhere for greater opportunity and personal and professional satisfaction.

Here's an example of what I'm getting at. I work with a large hospital chain that has more than 50 hospitals. The CEO feels that most everyone who works there is pessimistic about the future of health care—their Futureview is that the good old days are behind them and, as a result, optimism about the future is almost nonexistent. Not only does that sort of environment prove challenging in terms of retaining talented employees, but also what sort of atmosphere is it in which to encourage constructive change and innovation?

Anticipating Needs

We've already addressed how an Anticipatory Mindset can be pivotal to your ability to accurately anticipate opportunities of all sorts. That Anticipatory Mindset can also be exceedingly useful in a capacity to anticipate needs—on an organization-wide level as well as on an individual basis.

Just as you can leverage Hard Trends to gauge whether your organization has a shared and optimistic Futureview, so, too, can you use Hard Trends to develop a culture through which needs, problems, and disruptions can be identified and addressed before they occur.

Here's a scenario to illustrate how this can be applied. If you are selling a plan to build a new shopping mall to real estate investors, you can anticipate that they will be worried that brick-and-mortar retailers will soon be a thing of the past, that this might make it a bad investment. But by anticipating this problem, you can be prepared to point out that humans are social beings that will continue to have the need to get out from behind their computer and have a great physical experience, including delicious food, entertainment, and pleasant surprises. In addition, many will continue to have a need to actually see, feel, touch, or try on what they are interested in. The key is to design better experiences than they have had in the past and to build change into the design so that the mall can stay fresh and relevant.

Moreover, the customer of a shopping mall developer is often a retailer. Retailers, including online retailers such as Amazon, keep introducing new products. That mandates the need to educate consumers about those new products—something that often happens most effectively in brick-and-mortar outlets.

This ties in with one of the Eight Hard Trend Pathways to Innovation: mobility. Consumers will continue to have smarter smartphones as well as wearables that allow them to connect to just about everything. Along those lines, the mall could be designed to be an experiential destination that includes temporary mobile vendors offering new and exciting items as part of the mall experience. Accordingly, a consumer might want the mobile app for the mall or some other mobile application to let them know, in a personalized way, what's new and interesting there this week.

We're just talking about shopping malls, but anticipating customer needs can occur across the spectrum and does not have to involve technology directly. For example, a customer coming into your store to buy something may find just the item she wants. But, before pulling out her credit card, she pulls out her smartphone to do a little price comparison with other retailers. What if you had a guarantee that you'll match whatever price they can find on their phone? By anticipating their need for making certain they're getting the best deal they can, you're capturing greater sales.

Anticipating need can also be an internal issue. For instance, hospitals can anticipate the needs that will arise from the steadily growing use of health-related smartphone apps. Schools of all sorts can anticipate changes in their curriculum that will be needed to address the increased use of mobile technology by all student populations.

Anticipating needs allows organizations and individuals a means of identifying issues and problems before they occur. Not only does this eliminate the nightmare of having to react after the fact to many problems, but it also promotes the development of innovative products and services that address needs before they become genuine issues.

Again, it's not just about the development of new tools but also how those tools can be creatively used. For instance, mobile apps are everywhere these days. In and of themselves, they're nothing new. It's how they're designed to be used that represents the opportunity to anticipate and address a need. To illustrate, shopping apps are commonplace. But shoppers going into a large store are often still confronted by the logistics of trying to navigate aisle after aisle to locate the items they want. Anticipating that need, consider an app that, incorporating augmented reality, allows shoppers to see just where the shoes are, where the televisions are located, and the fastest route to the cold and flu medicine they prefer. Where's a customer representative who can provide assistance? Right over in aisle seven, three aisles over! Touch the app, and the customer rep is on his way over to assist you.

Failing Fast to Learn Faster

Many of our habits are hardwired with a Rearview Mirror Mindset. For instance, consider the approach that many take when something they're trying to do or achieve simply isn't going the way they expected. The traditional—even time-honored—mindset is to stay the course, continue to work on the problem, and never, ever admit defeat. If at first you don't succeed, try, try again.

In many instances, that's simply not the best mindset. Few things in this world come out perfectly. We are all going to experience failure regardless of how you define it, at some point in our lives—very likely, numerous times. It's valuable to acknowledge and plan for that reality.

It's also valuable to consider another salient principle of the AO Model. If failure happens, it happens fast.

Many companies, organizations, and individuals fail slowly. Consider a company that releases a product to disastrous feedback and reviews. What do they often do? Spend years tinkering, adjusting, redesigning, and making other efforts aimed at fixing something that, at its core, is pretty much unfixable. Another example is a company with a product or service that is being utterly disrupted by a competitor's innovation. What often happens? The product or service slogs on, despite the growing reality of its obsolescence and irrelevancy. Failing slow is an expensive (and unsuccessful) protection of the status quo. Just ask Kodak, Blockbuster, Dell, HP, and a host of other companies from the recent past!

On an individual level, have you ever hired somebody you sensed soon after they started working just wasn't going to fit in? Still, you kept them on, gave them things to practice, issues to work on and improve, only to realize two years down the road that they were a bad hire from the get-go.

Those and other examples underscore the value of Failing Fast. Not only does Failing Fast move you past the emotions and dynamics of failing, it helps you to learn faster. In other words, you interpret what happened, share what you've learned from the mistake, and move forward, rather than pointlessly wallowing in it.

Here, it's important to have metrics in place to determine when it's time to Fail Fast rather than trying to fix whatever the problem might be. One way to do this is to leverage Hard Trends. If a Hard Trend runs counter to what you're doing (or are planning on doing), that can be a reasonably reliable barometer that Failing Fast and moving on may be the most advisable course of action. Additionally, from a planning standpoint, it can be helpful to review plans on a regular basis, not only to ensure that your plans remain relevant but also to identify possible missteps that may warrant a strategy of Failing Fast.

Failing Fast also means communicating what you've learned. Let's say I run a company with 500 sales representatives. Salesperson #407 has tried something with several clients and failed. She then tried a different approach with another client and is now enjoying remarkable success. At the same time, Salesperson #202 is about to make the same mistake that #407 made repeatedly, simply because she was unaware of what her colleague had learned. If you don't share what you learn when you fail, you're effectively allowing someone else to replicate the same misstep. To make the most of the value of failing, let those around you in on what you've learned. The faster you fail, the faster you learn!

No one likes failure. But looked at one way, failure is only failure if you don't learn something valuable from the experience. Moreover, if you don't fail occasionally, you're not really trying to innovate. Choosing to fail slowly by default just puts you in a protective, defensive mode—one borne of reaction rather than anticipation. Far better and constructive to learn from our mistakes as quickly as possible and refocus our attention on leveraging the Hard Trends that are shaping both the present and the future.

Chapter 9

Elevate Planning to Accelerate Results

E very business has a strategic plan in place. Some, naturally enough, are more detailed than others. The goal of being anticipatory with regard to planning is not to discard plans but to craft them based on the Hard Trends and exponential changes that are shaping the future. By scanning for new disruptions and game changers, you can integrate this new knowledge to elevate the relevancy of your current plans and, at the same time, gain a new level of strategic advantage.

This allows Anticipatory Organizations to achieve greater levels of success faster than they might ever have thought possible and to see opportunities that they might well have missed.

When I consult with leadership teams, I'm not doing their planning for them—organizations of all sizes already have plans. Instead, I'm helping them use Hard and Soft Trends to see previously invisible opportunities that can lead to accelerated growth and game-changing advantage. The goal is to elevate their current plans and to drive innovation using exponential tools that yield transformational results.

High Value, Low Risk Opportunities at Greater Speed

It's not just what an organization knows or sees as they plan for the future. It's also the risks, disruptions, and game-changing opportunities that they don't see. Often, these merely slow down their progress.

Applying the principles of AO provides a new type of lens with which to view those factors and issues—and, from there, methodology to elevate and accelerate those plans that they've worked so diligently to develop. By adopting an Anticipatory Mindset, you can examine existing strategies with a fresh set of eyes.

More specifically, elevated planning based on the direction the future is headed involves several very beneficial components. First, as I touched on at the conclusion of chapter 8, it's an entirely new means of risk management. Understanding Hard and Soft Trends brings a sharper focus to the underlying reasoning and assumptions that are implicit in any plan. For instance, in reviewing a current plan, are there certain critical elements that are, in fact, high risk assumptions—Soft Trends based on Soft Assumptions? Identifying those points of concern and conducting the research to test the validity of the underlying assumptions allows for a shift in planning to yield more dependable assumptions.

That brings a greater level of risk management and certainty to any plan. Again, it's not a matter of tossing out all existing plans in favor of a complete redo or change of course. Instead, it's a more complete form of analysis and evaluation that allows you to identify problems and hurdles that can be addressed before they can derail a plan in its entirety.

Using the AO Model to elevate your planning also helps uncover significant opportunities that might have been previously overlooked or ignored. Again, identifying and understanding Hard and Soft Trends can help steer your attention to a major opportunity that, on the surface, might be all too easy to miss. For instance, by applying the Hard Trend of 3D printing, some European hospitals have introduced systems in which they print out 3D replicas of human body parts. More specifically, by scanning a patient's knee and then printing a personalized artificial knee to the exact specifications of the patient, a replacement knee is certain to be a perfect fit.

An additional benefit of applying the AO Model is accelerated results—not so much in terms of the time it takes to put a comprehensive plan together but the speed with which primary goals can be attained. Strategies that we've covered, such as Problem Skipping, use of Opposites, and Failing Fast to Learn Faster, can expedite the success of any plan, putting both short- and long-term objectives within reach far sooner than planning that doesn't leverage these and other components of the AO Model. For example, a midsized accounting firm used Hard Trends to pinpoint cybersecurity as an increasing problem for small and midsized companies. Accordingly, they identified a small cybersecurity company, which they subsequently acquired. They then introduced this as a new service to their clients. In less than a year, it became one of the fastest growing services they offer. In so doing, they used the AO Model to elevate the relevancy of their plans and accelerate their financial results.

It's also important to point out the value of a more inclusive perspective when it comes to planning. Normally, most people might see planning as a very top down sort of process—leadership devises the plan, and everyone else carries it out.

The reason this book isn't titled *The Anticipatory Individual* is that this is about creating a pervasive mindset—an attention to plans that takes hold throughout entire organizations. In an Anticipatory Organization, everyone is aware of how to separate Hard and Soft Trends and other elements of the AO Model. People use anticipatory words and phrases on a daily basis because they're part of the culture. In short, elevating planning, accelerating innovation, and transforming results becomes everyone's job.

Here are some questions that will help shift your plans toward greater relevance:

- When you look at whatever current plans you may have in place, are there any Hard or Soft Trends that you missed?

- Are your plans aligned with those Hard Trends that are shaping your industry and your products and services?

- Are you actively influencing Soft Trends to your advantage?

- Does your plan's success depend on Soft Trends that may be based on Soft Assumptions and, as a result, are needlessly volatile?

- What new tools might you be able to use to gain a competitive advantage or position yourself to reach goals faster than you may have anticipated?

- If an overall market is down, what Soft Trends can you influence to accelerate sales while everyone else is struggling? In any up market, how can you exceed others?

In Effect: Transformational Planning

Most planning is primarily incremental. That means planning with an expectation of deliberate, managed growth—5 percent increases over the next five years, maybe 10 percent or even 15 if you're fortunate. And, not surprisingly, incremental planning yields incremental results.

Incremental planning is good. You should continue to do this. But transformational planning can prove a powerful complement. Incremental planning can be very much out of sync with the extraordinary period of change and growth that we're in now. Think back to the Three Digital Accelerators—bandwidth, computing power, and digital storage—which are driving both exponential change and advantage. With those forces in place, why not leverage them in your planning? AO transformation planning—planning based on the Three Digital Accelerators, Hard and Soft Trends, and other factors—leads to elevated planning and accelerated innovation that produces transformational results, not merely incremental.

Transformational planning focuses on those extraordinary drivers and forces—such as the certainty and confidence that derive from identifying Hard Trends as well as malleable Soft Trends—to leverage planning in terms of both what is certain to occur as well as those forces that are open to influence and positive leverage. That pushes planning into a wholly different realm beyond conventional, incrementally crafted, and executed planning and allows you the option of becoming the disruptor and jumping ahead with much lower risk.

An example of this is Harken, a leading global manufacturer of rigging and hardware for sailboats of all sizes. Instead of doing the usual incremental planning and innovating that the vast majority of businesses do, they used the AO Model to do transformational planning and looked at how they could apply their expertise in completely different fields. They recognized they could use the same technology expertise they used for their most advanced customers, such as the America's Cup sailing team, to create a wholly new product line that could transform equipment used for rescue, fire, and safety. In addition, research showed them that steel cables being used for overhead cranes in construction were extremely heavy. Using much lighter lines that are stronger than steel developed by another company and leveraging their expertise in advanced lines and rigging, they could produce a stronger and far lighter alternative to those needlessly heavy construction cranes that are used in every major city all over the world. That's not incremental planning—that's transformational planning that can lead to transformational results.

Although, as I've discussed, a pervasive Anticipatory Mindset throughout an organization is a valuable component to elevate planning as a whole; so, too, are those people at the top of the organization critical to introducing and nurturing transformational planning and innovation. That begins at the C-suite. Of course, it's critical to have leaders within the C-suite who understand the disruptive opportunities both current and emerging technologies

> **"Technology is not a means to itself but a pathway to transforming all processes as well as creating new products and services. The result will be genuine transformation."**

represent. But it's no surprise that today's chief information officer (CIO) and chief technology officer (CTO) are both extremely busy dealing with legacy technology as well as trying to move their organizations toward new exponential technologies that are shaping the future, such as advanced cloud services and virtualization, just to name two.

Given all that they have to deal with, the problem is their current roles bog them down with far too much reaction and response and far too little anticipation. And, as we've said, being agile doesn't drive exponential innovation; it just helps them respond faster. Technology is not a means to itself but a pathway to transforming all processes as well as creating new products and services. The result will be genuine transformation.

Given that, far better for the leadership at the top to reflect a mindset that can see these revolutionary changes. Job descriptions as well as titles must be reexamined based on the Hard Trends shaping the future. For example, the CIO needs to take on the role of chief innovation officer (even if the formal title remains *chief information officer*). The goal is to direct and enable technology-driven innovation of all sorts at all levels. Alongside that, the CTO's current role is also losing relevance. A new, more relevant role would be chief transformation officer, a position charged with overseeing the ongoing transformation of every business process. Once again, the actual title does not have to change, but the job description does.

With that sort of future-focused leadership at the helm, the goal of transformational planning becomes an ongoing, broad-based effort that embodies the sort of elevated planning we've been discussing—planning that not merely accelerates success with greater risk management but which also produces transformational results.

Lastly, typically planning and innovation are distinctly separate functions handled by separate groups. The AO Model and Anticipatory Mindset and the resulting culture

> "The AO Model and Anticipatory Mindset and the resulting culture break down barriers to combine planning and innovation in a way that elevates and accelerates results."

break down those barriers to combine planning and innovation in a way that elevates and accelerates results.

Conduct a Pre-Mortem

All businesses and organizations are familiar with Postmortems. Although they can take various forms, these are generally reviews of product or service launches, projects, campaigns, and other activities that are held *after* they have been in place for a certain period of time, have been completed, or have failed. The idea is simple: Let's find out what went right, what went wrong, and what adjustments, if any, we should make moving forward.

Postmortems provide actionable insights based on lessons learned and are therefore very important. A close examination of any problem that was encountered is essential to future success. They're also a very effective form of education—as we pointed out earlier, even the worst mistake remains a complete mistake if you fail to learn anything from it. That's a powerful means of accelerating future results.

Since we learned the value of opposites in chapter 5, why not do the same here? Let's take a look at Pre-Mortems.

As the name might suggest, Pre-Mortems are very similar to Postmortems in that they involve careful analysis. But, unlike a Postmortem, which is the review of something after it has been done, a Pre-Mortem is used before a new product, service, or change is implemented, identifying predictable problems and all barriers to success, and then pre-solving them ahead of time. It is amazing how this can accelerate positive results and overall success.

On a simple level, a Pre-Mortem may involve some fairly basic questions. For instance, before implementing a new product, service, strategy, or imperative, what problems can we expect in implementation and execution? What objections will we encounter? That way, it's possible—in the case of predictable problems, to use one example—to pre-solve them before they have the chance to actually occur. A similar opportunity exists with positives—if we can anticipate that one aspect or element of a project or product is going to go particularly well, what steps can we take in advance to make sure that it happens and further leverage that success?

Here's a specific example of what I mean by that. When we were developing our Anticipatory Organization Learning System, we had a number of CEOs and other leaders from a broad array of industries test the system. We solicited their feedback prior to releasing the product. They told us what problems they foresaw in implementing the system in their organizations, what they liked, what they didn't like, what was confusing, and other valuable information. We then solved those predictable problems and made adjustments prior to launch.

In other words, it was an invaluable Pre-Mortem. In the end, we addressed problems before they had an opportunity to crop up and, in effect, actually become problems. That was an opposite strategy. Instead of building the system, selling it, and then finding out problems we would need to address, we pre-solved the problems before launch.

It worked like a charm. The system exceeded their expectations as well as our own, not to mention being named a Best Product of the Year! Just as important, those leaders and others with whom we worked prior to the release of the system became advocates—they not only embraced the value of an Anticipatory Mindset but also appreciated the fact that we took time to solicit and apply their input before we released the system to users.

This isn't to suggest that Postmortems are passé. Not at all. A review of a product or service once it's in use is exceedingly valuable—in fact, it's another aspect of elevating planning. Once you investigate how something is actually performing, you have the opportunity to make any necessary adjustments to help it function even better.

A Pre-Mortem takes that same approach, only proactively. To further elevate your planning, take the time to anticipate possible problems, drawbacks, and other aspects of any project, product, or service before they're implemented. That's a form of elevated planning that offers one of the most powerful benefits of anticipatory thinking—the opportunity to pre-solve problems before they occur.

Too Busy . . . Executing

A Pre-Mortem helps shift attention from a belief that many people and organizations cling to. As we've touched on before, it's all too common to assume that great execution is the most valuable competency there is. In many organizations' eyes, if you have a plan, all you need to do is execute well. Execution is extremely important, but in a world of rapid, exponential change, it can lead to a form of tunnel vision that could keep you from seeing game-changing disruptions and problems that could render your plan far less relevant or even obsolete before it's fully executed.

Blackberry executed quite well. So did HP, Sony, Dell, and many others. But what plan were they actually executing? As history has shown us, they may have been spot-on with execution, but in executing a plan for the future, by the time they got there, the future had changed. That's what digital disruption does—it changes the future. Technology has the ability to literally change reality. And so the question becomes this: "Are you going to adjust your plan to accommodate that 'new' future or continue with an old plan that places you in an obsolete future with fewer customers?"

It may seem a rather obvious observation, but the goal of planning is not the plan itself. It's about elevating the relevance of the plan as well as the organization in an ongoing and dynamic way. This is how you can gain a competitive advantage in a world of exponential change. In a word, it's about winning.

Strangely enough, that objective can be lost amid a focus on execution. The thinking often is this: Keep your head down. Work the plan. Give it time. If it takes years in the execution, stay the course. Along those lines, many companies and organizations map out multiyear plans—strategies that, as the name suggests, take several years or more for formal execution.

But, as I've stressed throughout this book, we're now in a period of rapid transformational change—a time when many of the things that we are all doing now were completely impossible just two years ago. Moreover, it also means there are things we'll be able to do two years from now that are impossible today.

One result is that plans that are solid now may be far less relevant or completely obsolete in just a year or two. Rather than just locking into the importance of execution, we need to use the AO Model to redefine how we execute. We need an ever-present Anticipatory Mindset, with our antennas up all the time, looking for both opportunities as well as potential disruptions. We also need to plan, based not just on what is possible today, but what the Hard Trends are showing us will be possible tomorrow and in the years ahead.

That level of awareness and anticipation can be very difficult if we've all got our heads down and are focused on merely executing the current plan. This doesn't mean a focus on execution isn't important— it is—but it's just as critical to focus on elevating the relevancy of our planning based on new, disruptive game changers as they emerge. In the context of our discussion in this chapter, what can you do to elevate your plans, to ensure they remain relevant? Further, what can you do to enhance risk management and, at the same time, accelerate results?

Why didn't a cab driver think of Uber? Why didn't Marriott or Sheraton come up with Airbnb? They were all too busy executing their plan. It's critical that, as we move forward, we take the blinders off as we execute so we don't engage in that same sort of understandable oversight.

Using Hard Trends to Sell Ideas

Implicit in this discussion of elevated planning and accelerated results is the importance of winning others over to the necessity and opportunities identified by anticipatory thinking. And that brings us to the topic of "selling" your ideas.

Everybody is selling something, in one way or another. Maybe you're trying to sell a product or service to a customer; maybe, on an internal level, you're trying to sell someone within your organization on the need for funding for a particular project.

Unfortunately, in our ongoing effort to sell, we often use opinions and debatable observations to try to win over others. Even if we don't see it ourselves, others listen to what we have to say and process it in the form of an opinion. In effect: "Well, this is just what Dan thinks. I know he thinks this is a good idea, but that's just one opinion. There are certainly plenty of others." And that reaction can lead to flat out rejection, refusal, or—at the very least—rigid skepticism.

Instead of offering what's construed as opinion, consider selling ideas in the context of future facts. When you hear a future fact, you know it. For instance, when you frame a request in light of the reality that Baby Boomers are getting older every day, that's not just an opinion or one person's perspective. It's a future fact that can't be argued—put another way, a Hard Truth that's going to happen, and that instantly puts you and the person you are talking to on the same page without any sort of debate.

I've used this method in my consulting activities as well as in thousands of speeches. It's amazing how it works. For instance, I might ask an audience: "There will be more governmental regulation concerning cybersecurity in the future. If anyone disagrees, raise your hand." Not one person puts their hand in the air, even in an audience of thousands with my remarks being translated into a number of different languages. That's because, to a person, they recognize a future fact, not some opinion Daniel Burrus is throwing out.

Take that idea and apply it to any situation in which you might be trying to sell someone something. Consider what Hard Trends—future facts—are going to impact the person *before* you meet with them. Ask yourself: "What is the pain or challenge that I know they are experiencing now that could be lessened or eliminated by agreeing to something that I'm requesting or offering?" Through that, your discussion will be based on future facts, rather than opinions, assumptions, or suppositions.

From there, given what you both know is going to happen, you can pinpoint your ideas and suggestions as a way to address those certainties. Perhaps the certainty is an aging sales force with many top performers retiring in the next several years. Given that that is bound to happen, what can you offer to best deal with that reality?

As we mentioned in chapter 6, one idea is the creation of internal, online communities of practice covering such areas as sales, IT, and customer service. The goal is to create a knowledge and wisdom base that younger as well as older colleagues can access as needed to train and grow their skills—perhaps through the development of a one-on-one or one-to-many mentoring network through which more experienced salespeople can pass their ready-to-use experience along directly to a younger staff member.

Not only does this framework of using Hard Trends establish a compelling case for whatever ideas you're selling, it also raises a primary caveat: the cost of saying no. Yes, money is tight and budgets are strained. But, given the certainty of the digital disruption and transformation and what we know will happen over the next several years, is saying no, in the end, going to be more expensive and costly in more ways than saying yes? What contracts, customers, and other types of business will be lost by ignoring these sorts of certainties? What major problems will result by saying no?

In other words, selling ideas based on the certainty of Hard Trends builds a powerful call to action rather than inaction. That creates the certainty with which prospects say yes. It is the ultimate closing tool.

Want to Accelerate? Slow Down First

Earlier in the chapter, we discussed a common problem. We are all so busy executing that we fail to pay sufficient attention to predictable problems and new disruptions that could impact our plans. It's a prevalent problem in many ways. Simply put: How can you do more with less and do it faster?

Ironically enough, there's an interesting solution, not only to moving past a limiting focus on execution but also in terms of embracing an Anticipatory Mindset as a whole.

In order to speed up, are you willing to slow down? To take the time to pull back on the reins and think and evaluate? As one saying has it:

Don't just take time to work *in* your business, take the time as well to work *on* your business.

Slowing down to speed up may seem like an odd suggestion. A recurring theme throughout this book has been the exploding acceleration in the rate of change. And that's true—we're no longer in a period of mere change; we're in the heart of out-and-out transformation, and it's happening faster all the time.

The obvious strategy for many would be to increase their rate of activity, speed up, and get things done faster. To which I would reply: If you're moving exponentially in the wrong direction, you're only going to get into trouble exponentially faster. Has the future changed while you're merely headed toward the "old" future?

That's the value of slowing down, taking the time on a regular basis to think, reevaluate planning, and make certain your plans and ideas are aligned with any Hard or Soft Trends that will impact your future. In effect, slowing down eventually allows you to accelerate and elevate your planning and execution all the more effectively.

Here's an example of how slowing down and taking the time for deliberate thinking and evaluation can accelerate your success. For years, the cloud was deemed insecure. For many, it was just too hands-off, even ethereal—far better to stick with what you are doing now. As a result, companies and organizations avoided migrating to a cloud-based strategy.

Once again, the future changed. Because of the exponential speed at which technology is changing, the decisions we make today might be obsolete in a year or two. A decision by many that the cloud was insecure might have been valid at the time, but holding on to this conclusion only kept them from seeing the shift that made the cloud more secure. In this case, organizations did their research on the cloud, deemed it insecure, and that was that. They felt they would be more secure with their current systems.

An Anticipatory Mindset understands the Three Digital Accelerators and the predictability of exponential change. An anticipatory leader doesn't limit decision-making merely to what exists. They also incorporate the future, using both the certainty of Hard Trends and the malleability of Soft Trends. In effect, many decisions made in the present are bound to be inaccurate and obsolete, often very quickly. That's because the future changes.

I saw the impact of holding on to an old decision too long at the highest levels. Time and again, major defense contractors—some of the most security-obsessed people on the planet—saw the cloud as insecure. That's because their decision derived from an analysis at a given point in time—not what was going to happen in the near future, thanks to Hard Trends, transformational drivers, and other forces. Needless to say, their attitude has shifted considerably in recent years. In so many words, today they are saying, "We need to get in the cloud; it's the only place that's secure now."

Seeing things beyond the confines of the present and revisiting technology-based decisions often to check their validity are essential elements of the AO Model. And, to help ensure the elevation and acceleration of planning that the anticipatory mind allows, it's essential to put on the brakes and slow down every now and then. It may seem contradictory, but slowing down on occasion allows you to make sure you are heading in the direction of the new future, the future your customers will be in. In other words—move faster in the right direction.

Chapter 10

Be the Disruptor, Not the Disrupted

When the word "disruption" is applied to the business world, it's focused on leapfrogging or upending historical products, services, processes, and models. For our purposes, that's a pretty fair description, and one that helps explain why so many organizations are unnerved by disruption. As the definition points out, disruption stops the "normal" flow of events and alters the status quo or current conditions. For many organizations, that's anything but positive news.

Still, disruption has occurred time and again throughout history and in a variety of ways. The cotton gin disrupted the means of picking cotton by hand that had been in place for centuries. The automobile disrupted horse-drawn carriages and other animal-powered means of transport. The railroads were an obvious disruptor. Interstate highways disrupted both industries and communities—if you were a small city and you weren't close to an interstate highway, you just lost a lot of traffic and, with it, a great deal of commerce.

In other words, disruption is not new. Given the explosion of technology and the ever-faster rate of change, what *is* new is the frequency, speed, and magnitude of disruption. For instance, when the cotton gin was invented, its impact wasn't immediate or instantly pervasive. It had to be manufactured, shipped via a relatively slow transportation infrastructure, and, of course, people had to be able to afford it. The same is true with other disruptions mentioned above. Railroads and highways both took a long time to be put into place and were exceedingly expensive in terms of investment and maintenance.

By contrast, consider the digital disruption that now occurs all the time. A new, revolutionary product is introduced and millions of customers snatch it up and begin using it within hours. Social media has been on fire for some time now with chatter about the "latest thing." At the same time, all those other products and forms of technology that preceded the new product are increasingly considered out of date—and in many cases rendered utterly obsolete.

Moreover, as I've addressed earlier, disruption no longer mandates the sort of infrastructure and financial resources that developments such as the railroad and interstate highway system required. An app developed by a college student in her dorm room, funded by Kickstarter, can be every bit as disruptive as any product devised by massive corporations. Disruption no longer requires enormous resources. Put another way, at this unique point in time, it's easier than it's ever been to be the disruptor.

Why Organizations Fear Disruption— and Why You Shouldn't

Given the capacity to disrupt and its potentially powerful and wide-ranging effects, instead of fearing it, why don't organizations actively pursue disruption more than they do?

One reason that many organizations would never consider being a disruptor in their field is their ongoing attention to other matters. Organizations in an established industry are all busy and aren't looking for what's next. We addressed this in the prior chapter, and it warrants a quick revisit. One of the most significant factors that discourages innovation—and, hence, being a disruptor—is being so busy that you never have time to get to it. It's the same scenario—keep your head down, keep working, stay on course. Unfortunately, being busy often guarantees that you will be disrupted, time and time again—provided, of course, you survive the first disruption!

Another reason is that disruption connotes risk—often, too much perceived risk for the leaders at the top to feel comfortable with. By contrast, the stereotype of the disruptor is the little startup coming in from the outside and completely shaking up the status quo. That, says prevailing wisdom, is the purview of the little guys with little to lose—and, like the focus on staying busy, another potentially dangerous pitfall.

Many organizations consistently misinterpret the function and flow of disruption. Many see it as a sort of one-hit wonder. When an organization or entire industry is disrupted, the reaction is often something like this: "Well, that's happened. We've got to figure out how to deal with this problem. We did a lot of bleeding, but we're still around." From there, many organizations promptly proceed to react and defend the turf that is the status quo, often spending exorbitant financial resources trying desperately to convince customers that their current product or service lines are still relevant and desirable.

Digital disruption is anything but a one-and-done proposition. It doesn't happen once. Instead, it comes in waves. To illustrate this, let's talk about one of our pathways to innovation: virtualization and, from there, the resulting disruption. Not very long ago, if a business needed several dozen servers, it had to buy them, configure them, and maintain them. Now, the same business can launch the same number of servers in less time than it takes to read this chapter. As you can see, disruptions along the same theme occur in waves that increase in speed, constantly shortening the intervening time between them. And, given our knowledge of the import of the Three Digital Accelerators, the speed and frequency of those waves are only going to increase.

These sorts of factors help explain why so many organizations view disruption with a good deal of anxiety. For one thing, their prevailing mindset is unduly locked on day-to-day execution—they don't strategically anticipate disruption. Moreover, they often see disruption as a one-and-done problem, rather than ongoing waves of new disruptions that are limited only by human imagination and appear faster as every year passes. That can make them hunker down all the more in their determination to protect and defend the status quo.

Consider the photography industry. When digital photography first came out, Kodak and other camera manufacturers viewed it as something of a fanciful toy, one that would come and go quickly. Kodak basically invented it, saw the result, then tucked it away. The fact that there were inherent limitations, such as fewer pixels and limited bandwidth that made sharing digital photos difficult, reinforced their conclusion that digital photography was a Soft Trend that would be a short-lived plaything. Of course, digital photography represented a Hard Trend that would not be locked away for long once the Three Digital Accelerators began to improve and spread in use and popularity at an exponential rate. In response, camera manufacturers scrambled to keep up by introducing cameras with digital capability, and that helped for a while. Only one problem: Thanks to dematerialization, convergence, and the Three Digital Accelerators, most pictures are now taken with a smartphone—yet another disruption.

Organizations with an Anticipatory Mindset don't view disruption as a problem to be held at arm's length, to be endured as best as possible when it occurs. Rather, they see the opportunity to be the disruptor.

Disruptor or Disrupted: You Have a Choice

The title of this chapter lays out a clear choice: You can either be the disruptor or the disrupted. From my vantage point, that's an exceedingly easy answer—it's always better to be the disruptor, leveraging predictable disruption to your advantage.

The reasons are compelling. First, it's far more advantageous to be the one exerting influence from the inside out, rather than merely reacting to external change and forces coming from the outside in.

That's one of the many benefits of building and nurturing an Anticipatory Mindset.

> **"It comes back to a bedrock truth that I always teach—** *If it can be done, it will be done, and if you don't do it, someone else will."*

Additionally, disruption is going to occur, regardless of whether we want it to or not. Is it safe to say that Kodak didn't want digital photography to take hold and spread as quickly and pervasively as it has? It really doesn't matter. The fact that they failed to see it as a Hard Trend and instead struggled desperately—and unsuccessfully—to maintain the status quo of traditional photography merely illustrates that denying the existence of disruption is foolish. It comes back to a bedrock truth that I always teach—*If it can be done, it will be done, and if you don't do it, someone else will.* Far better that it be you.

> Fighting to maintain the status quo instead of identifying and pursuing disruption will sink you deeper and deeper into a spiral of fruitless and frustrating reaction. When you struggle to protect and defend what you have, you only become further entrenched in your current business model and way of thinking—a position that can often lead to outright disaster.

Choosing to be a disruptor comes back to the bedrock of the overall AO model: being constantly on the lookout for both Hard Trend certainties as well as Soft Trends that are open to influence. An Anticipatory Organization is always scanning for trends that will disrupt both themselves and, in many cases, an entire industry, allowing them not only to proactively become the disruptor but also taking positive action in advance before an outside disruption occurs.

Leveraging Hard and Soft Trends to your advantage also mitigates the risk that many organizations consider a deal killer when it comes to innovation. As we've already established, using Hard Trends to jump ahead allows you to disrupt with low risk—or at least much lower risk—and uncover opportunities that lead your organization to accelerate growth and success.

Disruption can be particularly powerful when keeping an eye out for Hard Trends that are genuine game changers. Take 3D printing—a definite Hard Trend. Couple that with one of the Eight Hard Trend Pathways to Innovation that we cited earlier in a different context—dematerialization, or making things smaller. To that end, there's now a camera that can be 3D printed that is smaller than a fly's eye. Reading that, you might ask yourself, "Where would they want to put a camera that small?" Here are just a few possible answers: They could be sewn into the fabric or embedded in the badge worn by law enforcement officers, replacing the bulky cameras they have to manage now in the interest of safety. Or they could be embedded in the other side of a car's rearview mirror facing out to provide an instant record of everything that's occurring during a particular drive—a brand new feature! Put another way, if you're thinking game changer, you're thinking disruption.

A few additional issues regarding disruption warrant our attention. First, as I hinted at in my discussion of waves earlier in this chapter, disruption can prove particularly powerful if you avoid the mistake that many organizations make—viewing disruption as a one-and-done dynamic. Instead, take a broader view. If you've introduced a product or service that's proving disruptive, what can you do to take it to the next level? How can you, in effect, create the next wave that characterizes game-changing disruption? For instance, Google did this by embedding a tiny camera in a pair of glasses that allow the wearer to take a picture with the wink of an eye. The next iteration will not look like nerdy Google glasses but more like regular glasses.

Consistent with the idea of treating disruption as an opportunity rather than a problem, don't overlook the possibilities that come from a disruption that's introduced by someone else. Ask yourself, "Okay, here's this new product or service in our industry. How can we leverage that and bring it to a new level of disruption similar to disruptions we may have created ourselves? What if we don't see it as something that keeps us up at night rather than as an opportunity that lets us become the disruptor and lead instead of bleed?"

Always remember that you have a choice. You can either try to protect and defend the status quo, as numerous organizations have done—often to their demise—or you can embrace and extend game-changing Hard Trends to drive exponential innovation and extraordinary results.

The Need for Disruption

Many organizations often avoid pursuing disruption due to the stereotypes that the term suggests. "Disruptor" conjures up images of a science experiment—a few people in the dark, deep recesses of a laboratory or garage who have a fixed budget, no specific goal, and the freedom to pursue whatever they want.

That's hardly the case and surely not a prerequisite. Disruption is clearly a choice. Anyone with an Anticipatory Mindset—an awareness of the influence of Hard and Soft Trends and the other principles of the AO Model—can readily identify potential means of disruption. Moreover, if being anticipatory is part of an organization's culture, ideas for products, services, processes, and even industry, disruption can come from anyone.

But, disruption isn't limited to ideas. There are many industries, products, services, and other areas that, in fact, *need* disruption.

They can be readily identified. Often, organizations are remarkably deficient, offering inferior, outdated products, poor customer service, or an experience not personalized to customers' tastes or some other area in which they're clearly lacking. For example, how are the food, patient and customer service, and personalized care in your local hospital? Is the service at a nearby fast food outlet getting slower and less customer focused? Is your accountant helping you make future decisions by looking at your plans and the predictable impact in terms of tax and regulatory changes?

There's more. Education? It's loaded with potential for disruption. Shopping? The experience of shopping at a brick-and-mortar retail store is waiting for a new level of disruption, like what Apple did with its brick-and-mortar retail stores years ago. Apple essentially redefined the entire customer experience. Before that, salespeople at computer stores and most

> **"By reconsidering your business model with an eye toward the potential of disruption, you can be on the leading edge with the confidence and certainty Hard Trends can bring you."**

retail outlets were neither particularly knowledgeable nor passionate about what they were selling. Moreover, every store pretty much looked the same as the next. Apple changed all that. For one thing, staff members became knowledgeable advisors who were helping you choose the right solution rather than just hawking a product. Further, you could complete a transaction with a staff member using their card-reading iPhone. That effectively eliminated the need to wait in line to check out. Thanks to new transformational tools and a focus on planned disruption, we will see another reinvention of the customer experience as retail reinvents itself to remain relevant. Health care? Whether seeing your local family physician or a trip to the emergency room, health care is another industry ready for massive disruption on any number of levels. Likewise for insurance, transportation, manufacturing, construction, and countless other industries—all screaming for disruption.

This extensive list of fields that effectively need disruption ties into an anticipatory truth with which you're very familiar by now. If you don't do it, somebody else is going to—moreover, saying that it doesn't exist or "I'm not going to do anything about it" isn't going to make that need go away.

On the other hand, by reconsidering your business model with an eye toward the potential of disruption, you can be on the leading edge with the confidence and certainty Hard Trends can bring you.

ACCELERATE SUCCESS—
TRANSFORM RESULTS

Chapter 11

The Future Is about Maximizing Relationships

It's no great surprise that many people love their technology. With the remarkable developments we are witnessing and their capacity to transform our lives, our rapidly advancing access and attachment to technology of all sorts are easy to understand.

Sometimes, though, even I wonder if we may love it a bit too much.

Here's what I'm getting at. You're in a visually stunning location—say, the south of France or the Grand Canyon—a destination that people will happily travel thousands of miles to visit. And, while you're looking around, taking in all the beauty, you can't help but notice other people who happen to be there at the same time.

What are many of them doing? Staring down at their smartphone or even a tablet, hardly pausing to look up at all the amazing beauty that surrounds them. In fact, maybe you're one of them.

At first glance, it may seem that the world has gone wholly technical, to the exclusion of so many other things, be it natural surroundings, other people, what have you. And, given the emphasis on technology that has characterized much of this book, you would think that I, too, share the view that technology in our modern world is the name of the game.

The truth is, I don't hold that opinion in the least. This is still very much a human world. And no matter how far and how fast we progress technologically, it will remain a human world where positive relationships matter.

It's All about Relationships

The AO principle of Hard Trends identifies future certainties. Among the hundreds that have been identified, one clearly stands out in my mind: The number one certainty in this world is that the future is all about relationships.

Certainly, technology is advancing at an exponentially faster rate, increasing its varied capabilities at an astonishing speed. But all the technology in the world is secondary to interaction between people—constructive, trust-based interaction. Without that, what good is the most amazing technology?

Naturally, there are good relationships and bad relationships. Good relationships are based on high levels of trust; and trust, of course, has to be earned. Trust is earned through values, delivering on promises, honesty, integrity, mutual respect, and other similar core attributes.

Just as important, you never want to give people a reason to distrust you. Yet it happens all the time—not because people are evil or inherently distrustful, but because they don't consider the future ramifications of the actions they take today. It occurs constantly, particularly in organizations. An organization carefully builds a reputation and relationship with its customers over the course of many years. At some point, a change is implemented and that trust is shattered. Maybe the organization alters its privacy policy and starts selling customer information to other marketers. That can lead customers to say, "With this new policy, I'm not so sure I can trust them any more. And, if they change their policy now, they can change it again in the future." That can lead to the potentially devastating problem of customer turnover.

Here is a way to bolster trust using one of the core AO principles: You get the behavior you reward. For instance, instead of changing the privacy policy for everyone, change it for new customers only. With existing customers, let them know they can stick with the existing policy, but, if they agree to the new policy, they'll receive a discount or some other perk. In effect, you've given them a choice and are asking for their permission. Many will take the discount and accept the new policy—those that don't will still remain customers under the old policy.

Of course, trust is also an essential internal component to a great corporate culture. That's particularly true when it comes to change. No matter if you're the CEO, a departmental manager, or a supervisor, at some point you'll be implementing some form of change that will impact someone—quite possibly a lot of people, and quite possibly people from within the organization as well as outside of the organization.

Fortunately, using anticipatory thinking can be remarkably valuable to institute change that brings about the most positive results possible. *Before* implementing any form of change, just ask yourself: "What level of trust do I have between myself and the people affected by this change? Is it a high level of trust or something less? And, what will happen to trust if we implement change in the way we plan to implement it?"

This line of questioning can lead to some valuable insights. Maybe you'll realize that implementing the change in the way you are currently planning may compromise your current level of trust. If that looks likely, alter how you implement the change so that trust will not be comprised. Further, if anyone can think of a way to increase trust, reward them openly as a clear sign that you welcome any suggestion that will enhance trust.

Through the lens of the AO Model, trust between people can also be developed and strengthened when you gain a sense of people's attitudes about the past, present, and future. This happens through a technique that I refer to as a Time Travel Audit.

Conduct a Time Travel Audit

The first time I went to an advanced robotics lab, where they were testing a powered exoskeleton that a nurse could put on like a body suit and then lift a patient who weighed twice as much as the nurse into bed, I knew I was seeing the future—I was time traveling forward. Later that week, I visited a Tesla dealer and test-drove their latest SUV, the Model X. Again, it felt like I was experiencing the future. I decided to compare it to other high-end SUVs, so I test-drove the top luxury brand names. After experiencing the Tesla, I felt like I was time traveling backward. You and I time travel forward and backward all the time when you think of it this way.

Not surprisingly, people are wired differently when it comes to how they view the past, present, and future. However, understanding and uniting these mindsets to achieve a more future-focused organization can accelerate success. The key here is to figure out where one person is on the spectrum, and where you are as well, and respectfully walk forward together based on the Hard Trends that are shaping the future. The ability to know where an individual, a team, a division, or a customer is in time becomes an invaluable tool to increase your engagement, relevancy, and focus in your communications that can be used to achieve results faster. That's the powerful value of a Time Travel Audit. In this book, I will focus on how to apply this powerful concept to individuals, but the same methodology can be applied to teams, divisions, and customers.

At one end of the spectrum are people who remain most comfortable in the past. They aren't at ease with change and, in fact, often actively resist it.

That's not to say the past-oriented person is locked in the past interminably or is immune to recognizing the potential of the future.

Here's an example: I was speaking to the leaders of a large construction company a few years ago. Prior to my remarks, several of them gave me a heads-up. They told me about an older executive who had been in the organization for a number of years. He had done many great things throughout his career, had an extraordinary amount of knowledge about the industry, and was the author of several industry books. However, he was resistant to change and every sort of new technology—he wanted nothing to do with a smartphone or a tablet. As the company increasingly used new technology in planning and design and incorporated GPS to track vehicles as well as people, and mobile devices to help better coordinate employees in the field, he remained convinced that all these new tools were taking them down a very bad path—creating a very negative future. His stubbornness on the matter was very frustrating to his colleagues.

It was obvious to me—he had a past-oriented mindset. I knew that if I just went ahead and spoke to the group, he would just hunker down even more. So, prior to my remarks, I went over and chatted with him. Since I was very familiar with his work, we quickly bonded. He was comfortable talking about the past. Then I asked him if he had ever used any apps for smartphones or tablets. "No," he replied dismissively, "I don't use those things." I said I had used some apps that I had found really helpful and asked him if he'd like to see them—in other words, I asked permission. He said he'd look at them.

I showed an app that saved me time and needless hassles. He was amazed at how helpful it was. I showed him another, and he was just as impressed. After showing him three different apps, he announced he was going to get a smartphone!

The other leaders who had tipped me off called me two months later. They said the gentleman I had spoken to was a thoroughly changed man. He now fully embraced technology and—every bit as important—he was actually excited about the future. Instead of slowing down progress, they told me he was now helping the organization move forward faster than ever before.

Now, let's take a look at someone with a present-oriented mindset. They know the future is coming, but spend little time thinking about it because they are so busy dealing with things in the present. Rather than being anticipatory and proactive about change, they'll continue to treat change and disruption as a problem instead of an opportunity and a way to gain competitive advantage.

I know a professional services company whose in-house sales force is dominated by present-oriented thinkers. Whenever there is a disruption in their marketspace, or they are given new sales processes and tools, it takes them longer to embrace the new systems and ways of doing things because they don't see where the future is going and how these new tools will help them accelerate their success. They're far too locked in to putting out fires in the present and reacting to change to do otherwise. The key to helping them shift to an anticipatory, future-focused mindset is to acknowledge their current problem of being way too busy, and then walk them into the future with a new way of thinking about what they do. For example, many professional service companies set their fee based on time and materials, and most compete on price. By having them take a moment to think about how fast technology such as smartphones, tablets, and wearables, to name a few, has changed their personal lives, it is easy to convince them that exponential advances in technology will enable everyone to do more in less time every year. The mindset shift comes when you help them to see that if they bill for time, they will make less every year, unless they sell the value of what they do. Instead of trying to intimidate them into the future, you will get their permission to tell them more—walk them into the future.

Let's take a look at a future-oriented person. That's a person who's excited about where the future is going. She's excited about new tools and the opportunities they represent and is the first in line to adopt and begin using them. She can't wait until the next game-changing form of technology becomes available, even if she has to buy it herself. If she doesn't bring others into the future with her by jumping back into their time zone and using the anticipatory skills I have been teaching, she will eventually feel isolated and most likely look for work somewhere else. I saw that very thing happen with a large printing company whose leaders balked about adopting digital printing technology. Because the future-oriented employees did not start conversations by jumping into the owners' past-oriented mindsets and walk them into the future as we have discussed, nothing happened. As a result, the company's most innovative forward thinkers left to start their own digital printing company. Predictably, the past-oriented company they left behind saw their sales rapidly decline.

The inherent challenge and opportunity is to determine where a person is in time in relationship to you. For instance, let's say the person you report to is past oriented and you're future oriented. You're talking about a particular project, and you're framing it from your perspective: the future. Picture his reaction. His eyes glaze over a bit, and his thoughts are easy to read: "This is just too far out to be practical." Moreover, being more fixed on the past, your perspective is hard to visualize and relate to because it's way outside of his comfortable worldview. The key is to jump into the other person's time zone, in this case the past, and walk them into the future.

Let's explore a few more variations of how this can work for you. If you are past oriented, and the people you need to communicate or collaborate with are present oriented, you can still have a big disconnect. While your colleague may not be an early adopter of new tools and technology, at least he is up to date in using current tools and processes. On the other hand, because you have a past-oriented mindset, you believe the old saying "If it isn't broken, don't fix it," and therefore, you see using the latest processes and technology as a waste of time. This mindset will only hold you back in a world of transformational change. It will be important to have an open mind when talking to others and a commitment to learn the anticipatory skills in this book so that you can achieve your full potential.

Let's try another example. Let's say that you're really good at sales but, unlike my earlier example of professional services sales people, you're past oriented. It doesn't mean that you can't be successful. But it does mean that you'll have difficulty selling to people who are future oriented. It also means that you'll be very slow when it comes to using new tools that could allow you to increase your sales dramatically. However, you may not even notice this as you continue to hunker down using older processes and sales tools—and, in so doing, inadvertently hinder your success.

But, as I stressed at the outset of this chapter, communication and relationships with people are all important. The key here is to figure out where one person is on the spectrum, and where you are as well.

Let's explore another angle to this concept and how it can work. Let's say the person with whom you're trying to connect is past oriented. How can you tell? Obviously, you can listen to their opinions about technology and other time-anchored issues. You can also take note of the devices and tools they use. Maybe they use a flip phone. Maybe their television is an older model, large and boxy, unlike most current flat-panel models. All those signs point to a person who is past oriented.

If you're more oriented toward the future, it can be tempting to launch into an animated speech about all the cool things your smartphone can do or how handy your Amazon Echo is when you need a particular recipe at dinnertime. Unfortunately, this may cause them to hunker down all the more in the past or, at the very least, simply ignore most everything you have to say because they simply can't relate. Your perspective and values are simply too far removed from theirs.

Instead of asking them to enter your world, try entering theirs. For instance, if you're discussing a project or proposal, use a three-ring binder or printed documents to share the details. This creates a setting in which they feel comfortable and willing to connect.

But don't leave things at that. At the same time, you might say: "You know, I could show you this in my folder, but I also have a new tablet that has a way of showing many of these details in a 3D animated format. It's really quite something. Could I show it to you or do you want to just stay with the folder?" That overture may be all they need to agree to have a look at the tablet. With that, you've not only conducted a successful Time Travel Audit, but you've begun walking them into the future. You've got their permission and they're comfortable. They're freeing themselves to move forward.

The same holds true with someone who's more locked in on the present. They may be more at ease moving forward gradually than someone who's more past oriented, but smoothing the transition in every way possible makes the experience more comfortable—and, likely, more successful.

A Time Travel Audit isn't a force-feed of the future, nor is it meant to completely disregard the value that a past or current perspective can offer. But in conducting a Time Travel Audit, you're helping another person transition into a more balanced frame of mind, one in which they can gradually begin to value those elements of the future you already embrace.

The Time Travel Audit hits on a core benefit of the AO Model: accelerating success. By bringing a past- or present-focused person more into a future-focused mindset, you can ramp up innovation and accelerate progress toward organizational goals. People can gradually become more comfortable with new, powerful tools, and entire teams can move ahead faster once everyone is more focused on the future.

Just as important, you're building essential, powerful trust. By conducting a Time Travel Audit and jumping into their time zone as you begin to communicate, you're effectively telling someone that you value who they are, and that their insights and experience matter to you and the organization as a whole—and that a greater comfort level with the tools and potential of the future will only serve to boost those attributes even more.

Ending the War Between Young and Old

The heading for this section—which is, in fact, a major concept of the AO Model—might suggest a natural segue from the prior discussion of Time Travel Audits. In a nutshell, we assume that young people are more often the ones who understand the potential and tools of the future, and that it's usually the older ones who "just don't get it" and are needlessly locked in the past.

That's by no means true. I've known younger people who were utterly ensconced in the past. And by the same token, I've known many older people who are as future focused as anyone could possibly be. I know old people who are young and young people who are old. It's not their chronological age or how grey their hair is that matters—it's their mindset.

But, in terms of our discussion about trust and relationships, that's not to say there often isn't a chasm between the young and old that exists in organizations of all sorts. In fact, there often is, and it can be both substantial and destructive.

On the one hand, younger people within an organization can look on their older colleagues with a degree of disdain. They feel the older generation just doesn't understand new technology or how to use it; they're out of step and out of touch with all the changes that are happening. On the other hand, the older generation feels that young people think they know everything, yet they are lacking in so many key areas, including interpersonal communication skills (face-to-face).

> "The unspoken level of misunderstanding and mistrust between generations can have a very real effect on how the people within an organization view their future, which, in turn, will impact how they act in the present."

The unspoken level of misunderstanding and mistrust between generations can be more than a matter of differing attitudes. It can have a very real effect on how the people within an organization view their future, which, in turn, will impact how they act in the present.

For instance, a younger person may worry that the older people are running the show without taking into consideration what younger employees know about new technology. As a result, they're stuck in a company going nowhere. And older people may lose their enthusiasm for the future of the organization—with all these clueless young people moving up the career ladder, what might that future even look like?

It boils down to a lack of respect and, more significantly, a lack of trust. Assumptions are in play that can prove completely invalid and that undermine trust. Instead of a powerful, shared vision, employees have a different and often negative view of the future. I'm sure you can guess what type of future that will create.

A two-step process can address this. The first step is to have both the younger and older employee recognize each other's strengths and weaknesses. This results in a collaborative attitude, not to mention an increase in trust. The older generation's strength is knowledge and wisdom that come from years of experience. Their weakness is their lack of out-of-the-box thinking and knowledge of new technology. By contrast, the younger generation has yet to build any such "box," and they understand technology. Their drawback is a lack of experience.

The second step is to employ a Time Travel Audit. If, for instance, one of the issues that's increasing the gap between younger and older people in an organization is individuals' views of the past, present, and future, a Time Travel Audit can prove very effective in helping to bridge the gap and end a good deal of generational mistrust.

Look to embrace what all the people within an organization bring to the group. Younger people can leverage their strengths by offering perspectives, energy, and out-of-the-box insights that are a fresh departure from more established ways of thinking. Older people can leverage their experience, knowledge, and wisdom—strengths the young can't acquire by way of a seminar or college course, but which their older colleagues can share with them.

Carry that strategy of shared unity into action. For instance, if your organization is holding a very important strategic meeting where you're going to be making some key decisions, take a look at the attendee list in advance. Is it comprised exclusively of Baby Boomers? Think of the message that you may be conveying to younger employees—that the only way of making a significant contribution in this organization is to get old.

Instead, carefully select some young people to join you in the meeting. Not only can they offer feedback and insights that may not come from their older colleagues, but the inherent message is a powerful one to every young person throughout the organization: You know what? There's a future here. They actually want to hear what we have to say. We can make a significant difference now and in the future.

That also addresses the critical issue of attracting and keeping the best talent possible. If potential employees feel that working in your organization is like being trapped in a time machine traveling in reverse, it's going to be an enormous challenge to convince bright, talented employees of all ages that your organization offers much of a future.

Nor is it an issue of organizational age. I've worked with organizations whose history goes back more than a century, yet they maintain and promote a future-oriented Anticipatory Mindset and culture focused on transforming their company as well as their industry. It all depends on leadership and a commitment to elevating trust and a shared future focus.

Reward Desired Behaviors

If you're in any position that involves leadership or management, you're going to be implementing many changes that impact how employees carry out their functional roles. To make those changes both pervasive and effective, you're going to need buy in and positive execution from as many people within your organization as possible.

That said, it's puzzling that so many organizations fail to grasp an essential component of buy in and action concerning new methods and behaviors: You get the behavior you reward.

I mentioned this in passing in chapter 6. As you may recall, a major farm and garden equipment manufacturer wanted their dealers to become trusted advisors to potential customers—accordingly, they wanted to encourage the sale of more comprehensive, technology-focused solutions instead of merely individual products. There was one problem: Their compensation structure was not changed and remained tilted toward the sale of individual products that leadership wanted dealers to move away from. The solution was to adjust compensation to reward a consultative approach, and dealers would happily shift toward emphasizing more comprehensive solutions.

This illustrates the essential value of rewarding desired behavior. In one sense, it circles back to trust and value. You're cementing the sense of trust and value that comes when a new desired behavior is acknowledged and rewarded. Additionally, rewarding desired behavior can greatly boost a mindset and commitment to accelerating innovation. In the farm equipment manufacturer's case, this meant applying innovative thinking and solutions to its sales force.

Nor do rewards have to be purely monetary. Public recognition for a job well done is one such example. Additionally, if monetary rewards are simply not possible, ask those you wish to reward how they'd like to be rewarded. They may ask for additional free time to work on innovative projects or one day a week telecommuting from home.

Moreover, don't overlook the role of an "ideator" in rewarding desired behavior. An ideator is the person or group who devises the original idea for something—for instance, a new product or service innovation that others will most likely develop. The problem is by the time an idea turns into reality through extensive development, refinement, and other steps, the original ideator often can be completely forgotten.

Make certain that doesn't happen. Take steps to make certain that however long an idea may take to come to fruition, the ideator's role continues to be associated with the eventual outcome. That will serve to encourage everyone in your organization to share their best ideas to boost innovation—another desired behavior!

That said, take the time to review your reward structure to see if you are, in fact, rewarding new behaviors and creating what, in effect, is a negative reward for old behavior. In that way, you obtain the behavior you wish to encourage. In an environment where processes, objectives, and ways of thinking are rapidly transforming, rewarding new desired behaviors isn't an option but a strategic imperative.

Communicate and Collaborate

A dominant business mindset holds that we are in an Information Age and have been so for a number of years.

Now that we have become Information Age organizations, we need to continue to evolve to become Communication Age organizations: There's a significant difference between informing and communicating.

Informing is one-way. It's static and doesn't prompt any action. Communication, on the other hand, is two-way, dynamic, and does cause action. If I inform you, I've offered you information, but I don't necessarily know if you agree with me or what you intend to do with that information. If we communicate, there's a two-way dialogue and enhanced engagement, which may well provide me with answers to those questions.

Informing can actually impede moving anything ahead. We're drowning in information, but it may not be doing us all that much good. In fact, when I speak to audiences, I often ask them if their organizations are good at informing and communicating. The inevitable answer is: We're really at the top of our game when it comes to informing, but communicating is another matter entirely.

The follow-up question offers an equally intriguing answer: Do you need to be far better at communicating? Absolutely!

The core issue here is that we all need to become masters of communicating, not just masters of informing. For one thing, not only does communication result in action, it can also address significant, pervasive issues, such as the gap between young and old that we just discussed.

If an organization were more adept at communicating rather than just informing, they could easily anticipate that employees of all ages would interact and respond that much more effectively and constructively.

Further, we have more tools at our disposal with which to communicate than just smartphones and programs such as Skype or Face-Time: social media, with the emphasis on the word "social." These platforms go beyond just Twitter. For instance, I worked with an engineering firm that implemented its own version of an internal social media platform that allowed its more than 31,000 engineers to truly communicate—and, just as important, collaborate in a new and powerful way on a global scale.

Similar to the informing versus communicating comparison, cooperation and collaboration are also very different. In fact, many people and organizations mistakenly think they're collaborating when, in fact, they're really cooperating.

In a nutshell, you cooperate because you have to. Cooperation is based on scarcity. How can I protect my piece of the pie, shield and defend what's mine, when I have to compete with you? It's contractive and exclusive, something of an arm's length type of relationship that acts as another point of disconnect, slowing progress.

On the other hand, you collaborate because you choose to do so. Collaboration is tied to abundance—rather than fighting to keep your share of the pie intact, how can we work together to make a bigger pie for everyone, even if we're competitors? It's inclusive and expansive.

Merely competing can be a dangerous course, particularly when economic conditions are challenging. For instance, when I worked with major automotive suppliers, they said they were collaborating with manufacturers. Instead, they were merely cooperating, continuing to fight tooth and nail for their share of a shrinking amount of turf. When the economy dropped, many of those suppliers went out of business. Their relationships were built on a house of sand.

Collaboration, on the other hand, can enhance trust and greatly accelerate success. For instance, in technology, Apple, Microsoft,

Google, and others can attribute much of their early success to strategic partnerships with competitors. Likewise, pharmaceutical companies are increasingly collaborating to share resources and information to develop and distribute life-saving medications.

In fact, a favorite quote of mine from Abraham Lincoln summarizes this perfectly: "The best way to defeat an enemy is to make him a friend."

That circles back to the core message of this chapter. However exciting and heady the speed with which technology is advancing might be, it is human relationships that have always mattered most—and will continue to do so. This is not just an issue of technological advancement—it's people coming together to shape an exciting future by maximizing human resources and capital.

Chapter 12

Direct Your Future or
Someone Else Will

The title of this final chapter might suggest a very autonomous approach to the future. In effect, when it comes to the future, you'd better be the one calling the shots or you'll be at the mercy of someone else's decisions.

That's really not the message at all. In wrapping up our discussion of the Anticipatory Organization and its model of incorporating Hard Trends, Soft Trends, and other principles to anticipate the future with confidence, it's certainly an individually empowering moment. By applying the strategies in this model (and furthering your skills through practice using our AO Learning System), you've acquired knowledge and insight with which you can move forward, make bold decisions with great confidence, and have a proactive hand in determining your future.

But it's by no means a solitary moment. As I discussed in the prior chapter, the future is all about human relationships. That's very much the case with the AO Model. As you develop and nurture your Futureview, be certain that you both share and align it with those around you—after all, this book is called *The Anticipatory Organization* for a reason. Here we'll start by expanding your view of what an organization can encompass.

Direct Your Future by Sharing

As I've mentioned at various points throughout this book, most every organization has a strategic plan in place. It may seem counterintuitive, but to direct your future as well as that of your organization with confidence and certainty, it's essential that you don't keep those plans entirely under wraps.

That may run counter to your experience, not to mention your comfort level. While every organization develops and implements a strategic plan for moving forward, you don't necessarily spread it around to everyone within earshot. You likely don't share it with strategic partners or vendors. Nor, for that matter, do you likely share it with your customers. Instead, conventional thinking might suggest you make sure that customers buy your current products or services today, rather than sharing information with them about something exciting that's coming out in the future that's worth waiting for.

I can certainly understand that approach to customers, particularly in certain industries. Potentially discouraging someone from buying something today in anticipation of something better tomorrow may not make a great deal of strategic or financial sense. But withholding that plan from others—vendors, dealers, distributors, and others—is another matter entirely. And that may hold true with your customers as well.

This circles back to the essential value of collaboration and how it can be applied to cocreating the future together. When you work closely with someone, the last thing you want to deal with is a misaligned Futureview. Looked at in a different framework, if your organization's mindset has a future focus and your distributors have, for whatever reason, a past-oriented outlook, whatever strategic plans you may have developed stand to be constantly derailed—however inadvertently—by those who are not aligned accordingly.

Instead, it's far more productive and successful to collaborate and cocreate the future together with those your organization relies on, be they vendors, dealers, or even customers. To achieve that future, leverage the value of Time Travel Audits, not only to let your collaborators know

> "Knowledge increases in value when it's shared, not hoarded. There's power in sharing and cocreating. And that engenders trust."

what your Futureview is but to see where they are heading as well and to identify ways to align and accelerate each other's plans. In that way, you make certain you're all going in the same direction, using new and powerful tools, including the latest versions of augmented reality, virtualization, the cloud, and artificial intelligence, to name just a few.

This is also a means of extending your Futureview out to those around you. It's developing a refined Futureview based on the Hard Trends that are shaping the future and sharing it with others. Not only does it allow for more pervasive levels of certainty to accelerate success, but it also lets you collaborate with others to correlate your products and services to the Hard Trends that will impact all of us.

This doesn't mean you need to share everything. Rather, it's more an issue of not keeping a powerful direction and vision totally to yourself. Additionally, there's the "abundance factor" we addressed in the prior chapter. That means knowledge increases in value when it's shared, not hoarded. There's power in sharing and cocreating. And that engenders trust.

Here's an example. I was consulting with a major appliance manufacturer. As it happened, I had also done some work with some of the subsidiary industries and organizations with which they partnered— their support ecosystem, if you will. It was immediately clear that there were some major disconnects between this company and the varied people and organizations that were supporting them. Accordingly, one of the lynchpins in my work with this company was to better align their Futureview with those of these varied support entities. Had we not worked on that realignment, their future would have been characterized by various people and organizations going in widely disparate and often contradictory directions.

The same can hold true with customers. Like your partners, customers can see you with either a past or present mindset instead of a future mindset. It's not surprising, as they know the products they've been using forever. The flash point can come when a startup enters the field and picks off customers because they see you as the past and the young, innovative startup as the future.

In that sense, sharing your Futureview with customers is all about being anticipatory—knowing that there inevitably will be competitors who will try to steal your customer base. Therefore, it's important for you to share your future vision with customers, so they can see you have a powerful vision for the future derived from certainty. It's based on a direction that, when they hear it, they will recognize immediately and embrace.

Here's a personal experience. When I was looking for a new SUV, I test drove the latest models from BMW, Lexus, Mercedes, and others. When I tried the Tesla Model X, all the other cars seemed like the past. The Model X felt like the future.

I'm not alone in that reaction. When Tesla began taking preorders in 2016 for its entry-level Model 3, they quickly had more than a half million orders on the books. Why? People wanted to buy the future, not the past.

The idea is simple. Share your Futureview of your products and services: This is where we're going, this is how we see the future, and, if yours is aligned with ours, we can thrive together.

Change Is Only Going to Accelerate

Even though the tools and strategies of the Anticipatory Organization Model are designed to empower you with the competitive advantage of anticipatory thinking, there's no getting around the reality that there are still plenty of unknowns out there. For instance, I don't know when the next major cyberattack is going to take place, nor can I necessarily predict how the world's stock markets are going to move on a particular day. Of course, as technology continues to accelerate in its overall operating capabilities, we may be able to do a little bit better in anticipating these sorts of events today than we were able to yesterday. But the fact remains there will continue to be plenty of unknowns and uncertainties.

But unknowns and uncertainties don't empower me or you. It makes us hunker down and dig in more, protecting and defending the status quo. The principles of the AO system, on the other hand, are all about empowerment. This is about using what we do know, not what we don't know—the future facts, not the ifs and maybes—to actively shape the future.

This is what has always gotten me very excited on a personal level—actively directing the future, identifying those trends that we know will happen, and using them to our advantage. That's why the name of this chapter refers to shaping your future, a key benchmark of the AO Model, rather than just sitting back and letting the future unfold for itself—and with it, its potentially detrimental consequences.

Still, are there more disruptions coming? Certainly, and they're going to come in continually faster and more pervasive waves. (Don't forget the Three Digital Accelerators!) So, what's the goal? By accurately anticipating the future, you can see more than enough to make disruption your biggest competitive and personal advantage. As Abraham Lincoln alluded, you're turning change from an enemy into a friend. That all derives from the methodology that we've been laying out. It empowers you with the confidence to make bold moves because you're basing them on trends you know for certain will occur.

An accompanying strategy is the AO Model's impact on planning. Like

> **"By accurately anticipating the future, you can see more than enough to make disruption your biggest competitive and personal advantage."**

I mentioned earlier, everybody has a plan. But now, when we have a plan in place, not only is it based on the certainty and confidence that Hard and Soft Trends and other components of the AO Model afford, it's also a dynamic form of planning. It's not static. It's never at rest. It's constantly in motion, based on everyone within an organization—leadership, employees, partners, dealers, and others—scanning the horizon, always on the lookout with an Anticipatory Mindset.

Of course, there may be others watching the horizon as well. The difference is we have the binoculars afforded by AO strategies and principles. We have a clear distant view. We've got a way of seeing things way out in the distance, long before waves of change and disruption strike our shores, affording us time to take anticipatory action. Nor is it a matter of throwing out old plans that no longer seem to be effective. It's about adjusting those plans, based on our knowledge of the certainty of Hard Trends and the malleability of Soft Trends, which affords confidence in creating better outcomes.

If you want a more enlightened future, you'd better be working to make that happen. If you want a more human future, we'd better use technology to make it more human. The AO Model and system encourage an active shaping of the future to make the best outcomes possible.

Choose to Be Extraordinary

A book is an important vehicle to teach new principles, but it is not the only tool. I'm certain that the strategies and insights I've shared have inspired you to take action to develop an Anticipatory Mindset. To that end, I hope you continue with the development and application of your anticipatory skills through the use of another powerful, interactive tool we have developed for you, our accompanying AO Learning System. In this award-winning learning system, you'll find practical exercises and application tools that will allow you to apply and practice these principles within a personal framework so you can further appreciate how the AO Model applies to you and your life, both personally as well as professionally.

Still, I have the opportunity to share another belief of mine that underscores the optimism with which I view the future. I know that we all have the ability to do not just ordinary but, indeed, extraordinary things. Every one of us has the capacity to tap into something inside of us that is genuinely extraordinary. In fact, we can all decide we want to live an *ordinary* life or decide that we want to live an *extraordinary* life.

A popular mindset holds that people are born extraordinary. That's certainly true in some cases—an Einstein or Beethoven only comes along so often. But there are also millions of other people who, in their own way, are doing extraordinary things. For example, take Mother Theresa. When she was ten years old, was she walking around saying I'm going to grow up to be Mother Theresa and change the world? Of course not. But at some point in her life, she stopped doing ordinary things and started doing extraordinary things.

Phrased another way, she chose to be extraordinary every day. And you can do that very same thing.

Most people considered extraordinary have had a similar experience. It's really not all that complicated. They just stopped thinking and doing the ordinary and started thinking and doing the extraordinary. How do you do that? Well, the AO Model and learning system are certainly two components that can help people of all sorts move from the ordinary to the extraordinary.

It all boils down to what you do and think on a daily basis. Let's say you're a member of a business team, and you're about to ask a question. Before you even raise your hand, consider: What would an extraordinary person ask? If you think about that for just a few minutes, a much better question will come to mind. Ask that one instead! You're taking a short moment to elevate your thinking and your actions.

Try it. You'll be amazed. It's not a matter of being born extraordinary or being miraculously struck by some sort of epiphany or insight. It's a way of elevating your own actions to a new level just by taking a few minutes to think about them. Those daily thoughts and decisions, given the mindset of the AO Model, can blossom from ordinary into extraordinary, time and time again.

Here's what I can guarantee. After some time passes, people will be saying, "Wow, you're extraordinary!" Why are they saying that? Because you are. You're doing extraordinary things on a daily basis at a variety of levels. What would an extraordinary mother do today with her son or daughter? What would an extraordinary father do? What would an extraordinary husband do for his wife? What would an extraordinary CEO do for his company? What would an extraordinary manager do for his team?

Ultimately, you'll elevate what you do to amazing levels. You will be actively directing your future from the inside out with extraordinary thought and action. And it will have a profound impact on your future and those around you.

Making the AO Model an Everyday Habit

Having just completed *The Anticipatory Organization*, you've begun a rewarding journey toward developing an Anticipatory Mindset, one that will allow you to anticipate and shape the future with the utmost confidence.

So, with that focus on the future, it's appropriate to consider what your next steps might be.

No matter the specifics of your answer, I can only urge you to make elements of the AO Model an ongoing part of your everyday life. Whether it's using the concepts laid out in this book to identify Hard Trends or employing Problem Skipping to identify challenges and move forward with greater speed, an Anticipatory Mindset doesn't exist in the abstract—in its own way, it's a very real entity that needs ongoing use and practice to develop and apply successfully.

To that end, consider taking what you have learned to the next level with our award-winning Anticipatory Organization Learning System as a core component of your anticipatory skill development and training. Unlike a static book, its interactive video-based design will help you apply all of the principles to your exact role and function, as well as your personal life. There, not only will you revisit the central principles of the overall AO Model, but you'll be guided through rapid application tools, practice, and exercises designed to elevate and apply your anticipatory skills and abilities within the framework of your own personal experience. For more information, go to AnticipatoryLeader.com.

And true to the title of this book, look to build and foster an Anticipatory Mindset throughout your organization. As I've discussed, one person with the confidence to anticipate the future and arrive at decisions with great confidence is a powerful thing. The same mindset shared by the leadership and management of an entire organization creates an essential advantage to both survive and flourish in a future where great opportunities exist for those who can see them.

You can learn from the past, but you can't change it. What you can change is the future, based on the actions you take today. By anticipating problems, disruptions, and game-changing opportunities, you can shape the future in ways that were previously impossible.

By becoming an Anticipatory Organization—or one anticipatory individual—you can shape a positive future in truly extraordinary ways.

Acknowledgments

Every great invention, significant innovation, or worthwhile accomplishment owes its birth and existence to the creative process of *collaboration*. Nowhere is this truer than in the conception, drafting, and production of a book. I owe an incalculable debt of gratitude:

To Jennifer Metcalf, my VP of Marketing at Burrus Research, who has helped in developing both our learning system and in the reading of the manuscript in its various stages. She coordinated the whole project from start to finish and contributed in a thousand and one ways.

To my wife, Sharon, who brought her leadership and vision, along with her vast range of experience, insights, and perspective as an entrepreneur and CEO.

To the thousands of leaders around the world from Fortune 500 companies to start-ups who have learned from and applied the principles of our Anticipatory Organization Learning System to turn digital disruption and change into their biggest advantage. Their amazing stories of transformational results have inspired us to write this book and share the principles with you, our readers.

To the amazing team at Greenleaf Book Group who have been wonderful to work and collaborate with—you have helped us make this book even better.

About the Author

Daniel Burrus is considered one of the world's leading technology forecasters and innovation experts. He is the CEO of Burrus Research, a research and consulting firm that monitors global advances in technology-driven trends to help clients profit from technological, social, and business forces that are converging to create enormous, untapped opportunities.

Over the past 35 years, he has established a worldwide reputation for his exceptional record of accurately predicting the future of technological change and its direct impact on the business world.

He is a strategic advisor to executives from Fortune 500 companies, helping them to develop game-changing strategies based on his proven methodologies for capitalizing on technology innovations and their future impact. His client list includes companies such as GE, American Express, Google, Toshiba, Procter & Gamble, Honda, ExxonMobil, and IBM.

He is the author of seven books, including the *New York Times* and *Wall Street Journal* bestseller *Flash Foresight*, as well as the highly acclaimed *Technotrends*. He is also a featured writer with millions of weekly readers on the topics of innovation, change, and the future. He has been the featured subject of several PBS television specials and has appeared on programs such as CNN, Fox Business, and Bloomberg and is quoted in and writes for a variety of publications, including *Harvard Business Review*, *The Wall Street Journal*, *Financial Times*, *Fortune*, and *Forbes*.

He is a highly innovative entrepreneur who has founded and managed six businesses, three of which were national leaders in the United States in their first year.

The New York Times has referred to him as one of the top three business gurus in the highest demand as a speaker. He has delivered over 2,800 keynote speeches worldwide to audiences as large as 14,000. For more information on Daniel Burrus go to his website at www.burrus.com.

Appendix A

25 Proven Strategies to Shape the Future

To Elevate Planning, Accelerate Innovation, and Transform Results

1. Use Hard Trend certainties to transform planning.

2. Use malleable Soft Trends to influence the future.

3. Apply the Both/And Principle to elevate planning.

4. Use the certainty of Hard Trends to sell.

5. Elevate and align your Futureview with others based on the Hard Trends transforming the future.

6. Focus on transforming processes, products, and services.

7. Become the disruptor to accelerate results.

8. Use the Three Digital Accelerators to anticipate the velocity of change.

9. Implement both Everyday and Exponential Innovation to transform results.

10. Elevate trust to accelerate success.

11. End the war between young and old to enhance innovation and collaboration.

12. Apply the Eight Hard Trend Pathways to accelerate innovation.

13. Move beyond competition by Redefining and Reinventing products and services.

14. Perform Pre-Mortems to accelerate success.

15. Transform risk management using Hard Trends.

16. Apply the Law of Opposites to accelerate innovation and problem-solving.

17. Identify and pre-solve predictable problems to accelerate success.

18. Apply the Skip It Principle to move forward faster.

19. Become an Opportunity Manager who is anticipatory and agile.

20. Fail Fast to Learn Faster to accelerate success.

21. Anticipate customer needs to accelerate success.

22. Perform Time Travel Audits to elevate communications.

23. Reward desired behavior to accelerate success.

24. Transform how you communicate and collaborate.

25. Choose to be extraordinary on a daily basis to increase personal relevance and success.

Appendix B

Definition of Principles and Key Terms

Shared Definitions Create Strategic Advantage

Anticipatory Organization™: An Anticipatory Organization applies the methodology of separating Hard Trends that *will* happen from Soft Trends that *might* happen to its innovation and decision-making processes. Employees of an Anticipatory Organization understand that those who can see the future most accurately have the biggest advantage. They actively embrace the fact that many future disruptions, problems, and game-changing opportunities are predictable and represent unprecedented ways to gain advantage. Employees know that it's better to solve predictable problems before they happen, and that predictable future problems often represent the biggest opportunities. They know that being anticipatory means modifying plans to keep them relevant and keep from becoming obsolete before they are implemented, based on the Hard Trends that are shaping the future. They are confident and empowered by having a shared view of the future based on the Science of Certainty. (*See* Science of Certainty)

Anticipatory Mindset: People who value the power of actively shaping the future by applying the Anticipatory Organization Model to anticipate disruptions before they happen, turning disruption into a choice, and identifying problems and pre-solving them before they occur. They deliver results in the present, and they schedule time to scan the horizon for emerging opportunities to accelerate innovation and transform results.

Both/And Principle: To see the future of technology-driven change more accurately, it is important to apply the Both/And Principle. We tend to greet innovation with an either/or assumption; *either* we keep the old, *or* we get the new. But this is not an *either/or* world—it is a *Both/And* world: a world of paper *and* paperless, online *and* in-person, digital *and* analog, old media *and* new media, mainframes *and* smartphones. By *integrating* the old with the new in innovative ways, you can create higher value than either would have on their own. Legacy systems are not the problem; it's legacy thinking!

Burrus Law of Bandwidth: The Burrus Law of Digital Bandwidth, first introduced by Burrus in 1983, states that bandwidth will double every 18 months as the price drops by half. Bandwidth refers to the transmission capacity of an electronic communications device or system: the speed of data transfer. You may recall how long it took to download a large document in the mid-1990s. It was very slow compared to today's video streaming capabilities. (*See* Computing Power and Burrus Law of Digital Storage)

Burrus Law of Digital Storage: The Burrus Law of Digital Storage, first introduced by Burrus in 1983, states that digital storage will double every 18 months as the price drops by half. Digital storage refers to the method in which data is maintained, managed, and backed up. You may recall how large and expensive computer hard drives were in the mid-1990s compared to today's flash drives, smartphones, and virtual servers that store seemingly unlimited amounts of data. (*See* Computing Power and Burrus Law of Bandwidth)

Burrus Law of Opposites: The Burrus Law of Opposites, first introduced by Burrus in 1983, states that by taking a problem, a product, or a service, and flipping the core concept around in the opposite direction, invisible opportunities and innovative solutions will become visible, allowing you to both innovate and move forward faster. By looking in the opposite direction, where no one else is looking, you can see what no one else is seeing.

Certainty: Strategy based on certainty has low risk. Uncertainty can open the door to a sale, but certainty is the ultimate closing tool because it provides the confidence to say yes. (*See* Science of Certainty and Uncertainty)

Change: Change is to make or become different. It is incremental. What it was before the change resembles what it is after the change. (*See* Transformation)

Choose to Be Extraordinary: One of the most powerful ways to accelerate personal success, and the success of your organization, is to choose to be extraordinary on a daily basis. At some point in the life of an extraordinary person, they start doing things that ordinary people are not doing. The key to becoming *extra*ordinary is to realize that every day, you have a choice to do whatever you are about to do, in an extraordinary way. Before beginning an activity of any kind, spend a few minutes asking yourself what would an extraordinary person do, and then do that instead of what you were about to do. In time, people will be saying you are extraordinary, and that's because you are.

Computing Power: Moore's Law states that processing power, the speed at which a machine can perform an operation, doubles every 18 months as the price drops in half. For example, to go from a 5-megahertz chip to a 500-megahertz chip took 20 years. To double that took only eight months, and that happened years ago. The process of doubling creates both predictable and Exponential Change that starts out slowly and then rapidly builds. Moore's Law is tied to the processing power of the chips in our devices. At this point in time, the processors in our devices are not as important as the ability to use our devices to tap into supercomputers in the cloud. This is where exponential change will continue. Each advance in computing power creates amazing disruption and opportunity. (*See* Burrus Law of Bandwidth and Burrus Law of Digital Storage)

Convergence (Hard Trend Pathway to Innovation): You can converge features and functions just as we have done with smartphones, and you can also converge industries. You can see the future if you use Hard Trends to predict the industries that will converge, which creates new competition as well as new customers and strategic partners.

Cooperating versus Collaborating: Cooperating is a much lower-level activity than collaborating. You cooperate because you have to, and you collaborate because you want to. Cooperation is based on scarcity—"I want to protect and defend my piece of the pie," versus collaboration, which is based on abundance, meaning "How can we work together to create a bigger pie for everyone?" Cooperation is contractive and exclusive; collaboration is expansive and inclusive. Collaboration is a function of genuine communication where parties work together in a joint effort to create a desired result.

Cyclical Change: A cyclical change is any change that occurs in some orderly fashion in which the events constantly repeat (biological cycles, seasonal cycles, economic cycles), similar to a pendulum swinging back and forth. Economists are masters at using the cycles to predict the future. The trouble is they tend to ignore Linear and Exponential Change. (*See* Linear Change and Exponential Change)

Dematerialization (Hard Trend Pathway to Innovation): Demateri-alization allows us to find new ways to add value by reducing the size of many of the tools we use and the products we rely on by reducing the amount of material it takes to build them while improving their capacity and performance. You can find new ways to innovate by ask-ing the question "What would have greater value if it were smaller in size?" Knowing that we have the ability to increasingly make anything smaller becomes a powerful innovation strategy.

Demographic Hard Trends: These are Hard Trends that are driven by demographics such as aging Baby Boomers. A few examples include Baby Boomers retiring, which creates predictable problems and oppor-tunities, and Millennials who want to learn and work in different ways. (*See* Technology Hard Trends and Regulatory Hard Trends)

Economy of Abundance: The economy of abundance is defined as creating economic value and wealth by the production and consump-tion of unlimited, nonphysical things. Unlike the richest people of the 20th century who made their fortune extracting "scarce" resources from the earth, turning them into a product, and selling it to the masses, the richest people today have made their fortunes by creating software and services. Virtualization, the cloud, wireless networking, and advanced mobile devices are a few examples of tools that can be used to create economic abundance. (*See* Economy of Scarcity)

Economy of Scarcity: Historically, our economic model has been based on the production and consumption of physical goods and ser-vices where *every transaction depletes finite resources*. If I sell you an acre of land, a truckload of lumber, or a barrel of oil, my own supply as well as the source supply are now depleted by that same amount. Econom-ics is called the "dismal science" because it is the study of the ongoing process of depletion. (*See* Economy of Abundance)

Embrace and Extend: This strategy is about embracing the Hard Trends that *will* happen, even if they will disrupt your current products and services. Then, apply those forces of change to extend the life of your current cash cows and create new cash cows that will extend long into the future. (*See* Protect and Defend)

Everyday Innovation: When we think of innovation, we tend to think of the big innovations that disrupt industries or create a new product or service line. This type of innovation doesn't happen very often, has long time frames from ideation to implementation, and only a small percentage of all employees will be involved in the process. Everyday innovation empowers all employees, on a daily basis, to find inventive solutions to everyday problems by providing easy-to-use methods for rapid problem-solving, as well as a way to identify and pre-solve problems before they happen. It also is about using the Eight Pathways to Innovation as a way to make invisible opportunities for innovation visible.

Exponential Change: Exponential Change starts out slowly and then rapidly builds. An arithmetic change curve follows a sequence that starts with 1 followed by 2 and then 3. An Exponential Change demonstrates the process of doubling and starts out with a 1 followed by 2 then 4 then 8. Imagine taking a penny and doubling it every day. Tomorrow, you'd have $.02; the next day, $.04, then $.08, and so on. By the end of the week, you would have $.64. By the end of week two, it would have grown to $81.92. Not too exciting. But by day twenty-eight, just two weeks later, your pile of pennies would exceed $1 million; and by day 31, you would have more than $10 million. That's Exponential Change. (*See* Cyclical Change and Linear Change)

Exponential Innovation: This is a form of significant, disruptive innovation that accelerates at an exponential rate that can upend entire industries or create completely new products or services.

Fail Fast Principle: Part of living successfully in the future is embracing a new relationship with one of our most valuable and underappreciated resources: our failures. Our most valuable life lessons never come from our successes—they come from our failures. The biggest problem with failure is not that it's failure, but that we tend to fail in slow motion, dragging it out for years or even decades, which weighs us down and prevents us from moving forward. Learning to Fail Fast allows one to recognize failure quickly and act on it immediately, so that failure shifts from being a liability to being an asset. In fact, it becomes an essential tool for success.

Future Mindset: This describes people who look forward to new advancements in technology and the tools they use personally and professionally. They are aware of proposed changes in devices, software, and apps, as well as innovative applications for new tools. They have a strong willingness to experiment with the latest devices and software upgrades. They are generally first to acquire new technology. They have a worldview described as "The best days are yet to come" and tend to be impatient, thinking that things are changing too slowly. (*See* Present Mindset and Past Mindset)

Futureview Principle: The Futureview Principle states that how you view the future shapes your actions today, and your actions today will shape your future. Change your Futureview, and you will change your future. Your Futureview will determine the future you. Your future will be far less than it could be without elevating your Futureview based on the Hard Trends that are shaping it. It's clear that Blackberry had a different Futureview than Apple had. Blockbuster had a different Futureview than Netflix. These companies' Futureviews shaped their future. If one can elevate a Futureview based on the Hard Trends and transformational changes that are shaping the future, it will elevate the future of the individual and the organization. (*See* Shared Futureview)

Globalization (Hard Trend Pathway to Innovation): Globalization is made possible by technology. From ancient sailing ships, undersea telephone lines, and airplanes, to today's streaming multimedia communications, new technology enables new levels of globalization. There are also degrees and levels of globalization. An example of a lower level of globalization is a manufacturer that sells its products in markets throughout the world. A higher level of globalization is a manufacturer that customizes its products for the different markets around the world. Do your top executives often travel to other countries or are they from other counties? Both represent different levels of globalization.

Hard Assumption: A Hard Assumption is when we have "good data" that supports the underlying assumption of the Soft Trend. Soft Trends that are based on Hard Assumptions are more likely to happen, and, if you have a strategy that depends on this Soft Trend happening, your risk level is lower. (*See* Soft Assumption)

Hard Trend: A Hard Trend is a trend that will happen and is based on measurable, tangible, and fully predictable facts, events, or objects. Hard Trends cannot be changed. The three major categories of Hard Trends are Demographics, Government Regulations, and Technology. (*See* Soft Trend)

Informing versus Communicating: The Information Age is all about informing. Informing is static, it's one-way, it's passive, and it doesn't always cause action. The Communication Age is about communicating. Communicating is dynamic, it's two-way, it's engaging, and it usually causes action. A primary tool of the Communication Age is social media.

Interactivity (Hard Trend Pathway to Innovation): The increasing ability to interact with all of the different types of media we use has represented a gigantic leap that we're still just beginning to comprehend.

As we continue the process of making all of our media dynamic and interactive, we're gaining the ability to interface with everything in new and powerful ways.

Law of Bandwidth: (*See* Burrus Law of Bandwidth)

Law of Digital Storage: (*See* Burrus Law of Digital Storage)

Law of Opposites: (*See* Burrus Law of Opposites)

Linear Change: Unlike Cyclical Change, Linear Change is one-way and does not repeat. Linear Change is usually depicted on a graph as a straight line going in one direction. The Three Digital Accelerators take this one-way direction of change and accelerate it at an exponential rate, morphing this one-way Linear Change into an Exponential Change curve that starts out slow and then sweeps up at an increasing rate. (*See* Cyclical Change and Exponential Change)

Mobility (Hard Trend Pathway to Innovation): Mobility is enabled by the *hardware revolution* with increasingly smart devices such as smartphones, wearables, and tablets, and the *software revolution* with mobile apps that connect to increasingly capable supercomputers in the cloud, allowing people to live, work, and play from any place, at any time. Mobility will transform every business process.

Networking (Hard Trend Pathway to Innovation): We will continue to have an exponential growth of wired, fiber, and wireless networking that can increasingly connect people, places, and things. In addition, both tangible and virtual networking will exponentially grow. The more individuals we connect to the same network of ever-expanding bandwidth, the more diverse kinds of activities and services we can provide over that network, which increases the value as it brings down the cost.

Opportunity Manager: The majority of our time is spent putting out fires and reacting and responding to change, which is often referred to as crisis management. Opportunity Managers do spend time reacting and responding, but they also understand that the future is where we will all spend the rest of our lives. They embrace the need to spend time thinking about the future and planning for it. Opportunity Management starts with the practice of carving out at least one hour per week to think about and plan for the future. An Opportunity Manager spends time looking at the Hard Trends that will shape the future and takes action on the related opportunities.

Past Mindset: People who feel most comfortable with how things used to be, generally demonstrate resistance to change and usually delay using the latest technology because they think the tools and processes they have been using are proven and working well. They have a worldview described as "Things happen too fast," "The future doesn't look so good," or "The good old days are behind us." (*See* Present Mindset and Future Mindset)

Pre-Active: This means taking positive action *before* a future known event. (*See* Proactive)

Pre-Mortem: This is the action of identifying and eliminating predictable obstacles and problems that will slow or block the success of a plan, product, or service *before* beginning a project.

Present Mindset: This describes people who are comfortably working with current technology, but generally wait until new methods or devices are proven or implemented by others before using them. They demonstrate a willingness to stay current, and devote time trying to keep up. They have a worldview described as, "if it's not broken, don't fix it." (*See* Past Mindset and Future Mindset)

Proactive: Being proactive means taking positive action now. The problem with this term is that you will have to wait and see if the actions you took were, in reality, positive. (*See* Pre-Active)

Product Intelligence (Hard Trend Pathway to Innovation): This is the degree to which intelligence is added to any product. Machine-to-Machine (M2M) communications and the Internet of Things (IoT) will add networked sensors, communications, and, ultimately, intelligence to infrastructures, vehicles, farms, and much more.

Protect and Defend: This is the default strategy businesses of all sizes take when confronting an external change or disruption. They spend time and money protecting their current cash cow and defending the way "we have always done it." This often leads to failing slowly. (*See* Embrace and Extend)

Redefining and Reinventing: The strategy of seizing the opportunity to rewrite your own history—before it happens. Transformation is an accelerated, magnified force of change. Redefining and Reinventing is a way of harnessing that wild force and applying it to a product, a service, an industry, or a career. Transformation is a Hard Trend, while reinvention is a Soft Trend. Transformation is going to happen, all around us and also to us, whether we want it to or not. Reinvention, on the other hand, will happen only if we make the decision to do it—and if we don't do it, someone else will.

Regulatory Hard Trends: These are Hard Trends that are driven by government regulations and laws such as cyber security and environmental protection. For example, technology will increasingly allow us to improve the energy efficiency of our products, which will save money and the environment. Regulatory agencies will need to update their requirements and create new legislation governing these new capabilities. (*See* Technology Hard Trend and Demographic Hard Trend)

Science of Certainty: This describes a systematic body of knowledge defined by identifying the Hard Trends that *will* happen. Understanding the difference between Hard and Soft Trends allows us to separate future facts from hypothetical outcomes—future *maybes*. Personal or business strategy based on uncertainty has high risk. Strategy based on certainty has low risk. Uncertainty can open the door to a sale, but certainty is the ultimate closing tool because it provides the confidence to say yes. (*See* Hard Trends)

Shared Futureview: The Futureview principle can be applied to an organization in powerful ways. If employees have different Futureviews of the organization they work for, it will be more difficult to move forward faster in a productive way. In addition, there may be employees in an organization who create a lot of value and are planning to leave. What's the difference between those who plan to stay and those who plan to leave? It's their Futureview of staying with the company. The Futureview principle can apply to customers, suppliers, and vendors, as well. If they all have different Futureviews, it will be far more difficult to share the future together in a collaborative way. (*See* Futureview Principle)

Skip It Principle: The key to Problem Skipping is to understand that whatever challenge or problem you have, no matter how big it is, that's not it. The reason the problem or challenge is so big and seemingly unsolvable is that it's not defined correctly. By skipping the perceived problem, you can find the real problem and, better yet, the solution.

Soft Assumption: A Soft Assumption is not based on research or data. It's based on an opinion or gut-level instinct. A Soft Trend based on a Soft Assumption is far less likely to happen, and, if you have a strategy that depends on this trend happening, your risk level is very high, and you can get into trouble very fast. (*See* Soft Trend and Hard Assumption)

Soft Trend: A Soft Trend is a trend that might happen and is based on an assumption that looks valid in the present, and it may be likely to happen, but it is not a future fact. Soft Trends can be changed. They are based on either a Hard Assumption, making the Soft Trend more likely to happen, or a Soft Assumption, making it far less likely to happen. (*See* Hard Assumption and Soft Assumption)

Technology Hard Trends: These are Hard Trends that are driven by technology. The increasing use of biometrics such as fingerprints and facial recognition for security and the increasing use of cloud computing by organizations of all sizes are good examples of Technology Hard Trends. (*See* Regulatory Hard Trend and Demographic Hard Trend)

Three Digital Accelerators: The exponential growth in computing power, digital storage, and bandwidth represent the Three Digital Accelerators. Burrus Research has been tracking all three since 1983, and all have been advancing in a very predictable way over the past 30 years and have been used to create accurate time frames for technology-driven change and transformation. Every business process is directly influenced by all three of the accelerators. Hard Trends define "what" will happen and the Three Digital Accelerators provide the "when." At this point, they are driving the transformation of every business process. (*See* Computing Power, Burrus Law of Bandwidth, and Burrus Law of Digital Storage)

Time Travel Audit: This is a Time-Oriented Mindset Assessment, which can be used to determine whether an individual has a past, present, or future mindset. Knowing the orientation of an employee, customer, or any individual helps leaders and teams understand how to increase communication, collaboration, and results inside organizations. When you know the mindset orientation of the people you are interfacing with, you can mentally meet them in their time orientation and move them into a more beneficial time orientation without alienating them. (*See* Past Mindset, Present Mindset, and Future Mindset)

Transformation: Transformation means doing something utterly and radically different. Transformation is an accelerated, magnified force of change. In a sense, transformation is a Hard Trend. Technology-driven transformation is going to happen to us and all around us, whether we want it to or not. (*See* Change)

Trust: All good relationships are based on trust, and trust is earned through values such as delivering on promises, honesty, and integrity. Trust means having a firm belief in the integrity, ability, or character of a person or thing, as well as the confidence or reliance of a person or thing. Both large and small companies can inadvertently undermine trust, or worse yet, teach their customers *not* to trust them. The key to success now and in the future is to strategically consider the impact any change will have on trust before implementing the change. Elevate trust whenever possible.

Uncertainty: We live in an uncertain world. Strategy based on uncertainty has high risk. Uncertainty often opens the door to a sale, but, if the potential customer is uncertain at the end of the sales process, it is highly likely the sale will be lost. (*See* Science of Certainty and Hard Trends)

Virtualization (Hard Trend Pathway to Innovation): Virtualization allows us to create on-demand services. Software can be virtualized, so you don't have to own, host, or manage it. Payment is made for the number of users who use the software. This is known as Software-as-a-Service (SaaS). SalesForce.com was an early example. We can also virtualize services such as collaboration, as well as any IT infrastructure including servers, private clouds, and networks.

Appendix C

Anticipatory Organization Video-Based Learning System

This book is designed to be a complementary component to our Anticipatory Organization Learning System. Unlike a book that is static, the learning system is interactive and dynamic, teaching you how to apply each concept to your exact situation and job function. If you have read this book and want to learn how to rapidly apply each concept to the work that you do in a dynamic, interactive way, I highly recommend our Anticipatory Organization Learning System. For more information, go to AnticipatoryLeader.com.

- ✓ Top Ten Product of the Year award winner
- ✓ A proven track record that generates results
- ✓ Has transformed how organizations of all sizes plan and innovate

Anticipatory Organization Learning System Features

- **Each lesson starts with a short, single-concept video followed by a rapid application activity designed to deliver results**: The sooner a lesson is applied to everyday activities; the more it becomes a part of the learner's everyday mindset. After each short 3–5 minute single-concept video, the learner applies what they have learned to the work they do regardless of their position.

- **Results-driven learning**: Benefits will be seen immediately, because the learner has to apply each lesson to the work they do. Learners don't have to wait until they finish the entire course before they see results.

- **We directly link planning to innovation**: A direct result of learning to be anticipatory is that it fosters two key areas of innovation: *Everyday Innovation*, where individuals learn to predict and pre-solve problems with inventive solutions, and *Exponential Innovation*, where individuals and teams learn to turn predictable disruption into game-changing advantages.

- **Next generation learning system**: We examined other best-in-class training systems from both large and small companies so that we could get a baseline to develop our next generation Anticipatory Organization™ Learning System.

- **We teach at all levels of the cognitive domain**: Unlike the vast majority of learning systems that only teach in the lower levels of Bloom's Taxonomy of the Cognitive Domain (remembering and understanding), our lessons have the learner use all of the higher levels, which include applying, analyzing, evaluating, and creating.

- **Learners develop an anticipatory mindset**: We are teaching a new competency, the ability to anticipate, which elevates decisions and accelerates results.

Benefits of the Anticipatory Organization Video-Based Learning System

You will learn to

- Anticipate disruptions, problems, and game-changing opportunities.

- Use the certainty of Hard Trends to sell your ideas.

- Jump ahead of the competition with low risk and the confidence that certainty offers to actively shape the future.

- Identify and pre-solve predictable problems *before* they happen.

- Increase personal and professional relevance based on the Hard Trends that are shaping the future.

- Skip problems and barriers to succeed faster.

- Accelerate innovation by using a set of tools to help you practice Everyday Innovation.

- Drive Exponential Innovation by using the Eight Hard Trend Pathways to Innovation.

- Elevate your Futureview based on the forces that will shape the future, and align it with others.

What AO Learning System Users Are Saying:

"The Anticipatory Organization Learning System helps establish a mindset, a common language, and eventually a culture of being anticipatory for our clients. By making this anticipatory skillset a core strength of our teams, it brings creative and new ideas that make us more valuable to our clients, and it creates a game changer for our firm."

—Joey Havens, Executive Partner, HORNE LLP

"The Anticipatory Organization Learning System provides a solid framework for how current and future leaders can learn to be better at identifying opportunities and shape decisions in a dynamic environment."

—William Bender, Lt. General, CIO, United States Air Force

"The Anticipatory Organization Learning System provides a solid framework for transforming an organization from being reactive to anticipatory. Learning how to anticipate disruptions and new opportunities is extremely important now and in the years ahead."

**—Anoop N. Mehta, President,
SSAI**

"The AO Learning System has allowed us to efficiently train over 200 of our top leaders, and, as a result, we have significantly elevated our company's strategic plans. We have also accelerated our investments in specific technologies and new products, which has given us a significant new competitive advantage."

—Jim McIntyre, President and CEO, Greenheck Group

"Every one of our partners went through the AO Learning System and it's outstanding, we heartily recommend it. Undergoing this mind shift transforms you from your current role to an elite advisor—capable of adding tremendous value to clients and dramatically increasing your marketability."

—Ian Welhman, Partner, HaydenRock Solutions

"The Anticipatory Organization Learning System (AO) has enabled our firm to understand a whole new way of helping our clients. We have trained our entire staff to help our clients identify Hard and Soft Trends, which effect their businesses or their personal life, and how to address them. With the rapid changes in technology in today's world, AO gives us a way to address changes, realize disruptions before they happen, and help clients in new and powerful ways."

—Allen P. DeLeon, Partner, DeLeon and Stang

"Even though you access the course through your computer, it is nothing like computer-based training (CBT). It is more like watching a number of great TED talks, and, after each short video, you help the learner apply the concepts to their role. It changes how you view strategy and leadership by targeting how to think instead of telling you what to think. You are able to distill some very complex concepts, frame them in a manageable and meaningful way, and allow the user to tailor the lessons to their own field. It resonated with me far better than I expected a course delivered through this format ever could. Well done!"

—Adam Dalson, Major, United States Air Force

"The beauty of the Anticipatory Organization Learning System is that it actually gives you a set of tools to harness the Hard Trends that are shaping the future and use them to create new value for your firm and your clients."

—Daniel Hood, Editor-in-Chief, *Accounting Today*

For more information please visit
www.burrus.com or www.AnticipatoryLeader.com

Index

 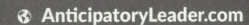